Supporting Gender Diversity in Early Childhood Classrooms

of related interest

How to Transform Your School into an LGBT+ Friendly Place
A Practical Guide for Nursery, Primary and Secondary Teachers
Dr Elly Barnes MBE and Dr Anna Carlile
ISBN 978 1 78592 349 4
eISBN 978 1 78450 684 1

Becoming an Ally to the Gender-Expansive Child
A Guide for Parents and Carers
Anna Bianchi
ISBN 978 1 78592 051 6
eISBN 978 1 78450 305 5

A Practical Guide to Gender Diversity and Sexuality in Early Years
Deborah Price
ISBN 978 1 78592 289 3
eISBN 978 1 78450 594 3

Gender Equality in Primary Schools
A Guide for Teachers
Helen Griffin
ISBN 978 1 78592 340 1
eISBN 978 1 78450 661 2

Can I tell you about Gender Diversity?
A guide for friends, family and professionals
CJ Atkinson
Illustrated by Olly Pike
ISBN 978 1 78592 105 6
eISBN 978 1 78450 367 3
Can I tell you about…? Series

Supporting Gender Diversity in Early Childhood Classrooms

A Practical Guide

Encian Pastel, Katie Steele, Julie Nicholson,
Cyndi Maurer, Julia Hennock, Jonathan Julian,
Tess Unger, and Nathanael Flynn

Jessica Kingsley *Publishers*
London and Philadelphia

First published in 2019
by Jessica Kingsley Publishers
73 Collier Street
London N1 9BE, UK
and
400 Market Street, Suite 400
Philadelphia, PA 19106, USA

www.jkp.com

Library of Congress Cataloging in Publication Data
A CIP catalog record for this book is available from the Library of Congress

British Library Cataloguing in Publication Data
A CIP catalogue record for this book is available from the British Library

ISBN 978 1 78592 819 2
eISBN 978 1 78450 914 9

Printed and bound in Great Britain

Contents

Introduction

Lucien is a five-year-old child in a preschool classroom in Northern California. Every day, Lucien comes to school wearing clothing marketed for boys, with commercial images of cars and spaceships and dinosaurs. Lucien enters the classroom and hangs a lunchbox emblazoned with images of starships and laser weapons, on its hook but they are hidden inside of a pink Barbie tote bag. This is how lunch comes to school every day.

Lucien then heads to the costume area. Every day, Lucien either covers or replaces the cars, dinosaurs, and spaceships with one of two outfits: a pink sparkly "princess" dress or a velvety leopard bodysuit. Lucien spends most of the day in costume until outside time, when costumes must remain in the classroom. Reluctantly, Lucien returns the pink sparkles or catsuit to the costume box.

Outside time is full of sand and water and dirt, and sometimes children come in for lunchtime needing to change into clean and dry clothing from their cubbies. One day, Lucien tells Teacher Heather, "Mom forgot to put clothes in my cubby, so I need to borrow school clothes." Heather opens the closet and looks at the two extra clothes bins labeled "Boys" and "Girls." Heather looks at Lucien for a moment, struggling a bit with which clothes Lucien would choose. She puts both bins on the table. For a moment, Lucien looks confused. Then, with eyes wide, Lucien asks: "I...can...choose?" Heather smiles and says, "Yes, but let's do it quickly because lunch has already begun."

Lucien does not get dressed quickly.

Lucien tries on half a dozen combinations, asking Teacher Heather: "Should I wear the rainbow pony shirt with the purple pants? Or the kitty leggings?" Finally, Lucien settles on an outfit and, after a happy day of pretending to be sisters with best friend Emma, wears the clothes home. The next day, Lucien's mom brings in the freshly laundered borrowed clothes, along with a stack from home for the Lucien's cubby. They are all dinosaurs and cars and spaceships. After outside time, Heather sees Lucien stuff both the new, clean clothes from home and dirty clothes behind a bench. "Teacher Heather," Lucien says happily, "I don't have any clothes. Can I have school clothes again?"

Maybe you picked up this book because you work with or know a child like Lucien. Most early childhood professionals are familiar with young children who blur gender lines, or defy them altogether. Maybe you're familiar with the term transgender and with thinking outside the box around gender norms and identities, but you're not quite sure how to do this in your childcare center. Perhaps you yourself are transgender, and you want to work towards making the preschool where you work more gender inclusive but don't know where to start. Or maybe this is your first genuine introduction to gender diversity, and you're really not sure where this book is going to take you. However, you found yourself here and whatever your level of familiarity with the subject, we hope to provide you with support and direction for making your early childhood environment a space where all children feel safe, seen, and respected for who they are.

Why do we need a book on supporting gender diversity in early childhood education?

The last few years have brought increasing visibility and media attention to the topic of gender diversity. There have been a range of newspaper articles and television shows aimed at increasing public awareness about the daily lives of transgender and gender expansive youth and adults with the idea that increased visibility will support greater understanding, empathy, and respect.

At the same time, there is still a stigma against breaking gender norms and rules. This stigma is reflected in several U.S. states passing or trying to pass legislation preventing transgender adults and students from using the restrooms most closely aligned with their identities. As of the writing of this book (October 2018), the U.S. federal government is working to define sex and gender as being strictly binary (male or female), dependent only on genitals or genetic testing done at birth, and unchangeable from a legal standpoint despite growing research that this kind of definition is insufficient and inaccurate[1]. If successful, this move would define transgender people out of existence in federal law in the U.S. Despite the increased attention, both positive and negative, the majority of the conversation about transgender identities offers little to no mention of the experiences of very young children even though our identities and our basic understandings of gender form as infants, toddlers, and preschoolers.

Many transgender and gender expansive adults report that they were aware of their feelings regarding gender as young as 2–3 years of age (Pyne, 2014). We also know that outpatient clinics specializing in working with transgender and gender expansive (TGE) children have seen referrals and client bases triple over the past 30 years (de Vries & Cohen-Kettenis, 2012; Keo-Meier & Ehrensaft, 2018; Zucker *et al.*, 2008).

> Keo-Meier and Ehrensaft (2018) coined the acronym **TGE children** to refer to "all children who challenge and explore gender identity and gender expressions" (p. 8). TGE stands for **transgender** and/or **gender expansive**. Both of these terms are defined in the Gender Vocabulary section in Chapter 1.

Current efforts to support **TGE children** generally begin when they are in elementary school at the earliest but usually much later. Very little, if any, emphasis is given to the early childhood years (birth to five) when children's gender awareness first emerges (Mallon & DeCrescenzo, 2006; Petty, 2010). In those first five years, children are developing awareness about how gender is understood in their families, communities, and society. These ideas will affect their understanding of gender throughout their lives including in their own identity development. (See section, "Why Early Childhood is such an Important Time to Talk about Gender Diversity" at the end of Chapter 1 for a breakdown of developmental gender milestones by age, and corresponding research.)

Young TGE children are often in early learning programs with teachers, providers, and peers who do not understand their feelings about gender and the types of support, encouragement, acknowledgment, and respect they need in order to confidently be who they are. Early childhood professionals do not receive information in their coursework or professional development activities to help them understand TGE young children or how they can create gender inclusive environments that support the gender health of all children.

There is great urgency for early childhood teachers and providers to learn how to support gender diversity and gender health for all children and especially for TGE children. Why is this such an urgent need?

Transgender and gender expansive children are at a high risk for violence and self-harm. The ideas and actions of this book are grand, sweeping, and controversial. They involve significant amounts of personal and institutional work. The question will naturally arise as to why it is necessary. Why should you and your co-workers put in all this effort? We deeply believe that the real answer to this question is that it is simply the right thing to do. This work is how we can truly honor, support, and empower all young children. It is the right thing to do to trust children and to believe them when they tell us who they are, and that is enough reason for us. However, there is also a sadder truth and a more compelling reason for some to become engaged in this work, and that is the simple fact that children are being harmed by the way things currently are. Indeed, many children have been lost forever to rigid and binary gender rules and the ways our society enforces them.

In 2016, the National Center for Transgender Equality (NCTE) published findings from the largest survey of transgender individuals ever conducted, with almost 28,000 respondents. This survey detailed the incredible amount of discrimination, violence, and injustice faced by the transgender community. While the report outlined negative effects of anti-transgender discrimination across every aspect of life, perhaps the most sobering statistic was this: "40% of respondents have attempted suicide in their lifetime—nearly nine times the attempted suicide rate in the U.S. population (4.6%)" (James *et al.*, 2016, p. 5). Of those respondents who had attempted suicide, 34% reported that their first attempt was before the age of 14 (p. 115). In addition to self-harm motivated by stigma and shame, transgender individuals face staggering amounts of violence from others. In 2017, the National Coalition of Anti-Violence Programs recorded 27 hate-related homicides of TGE individuals in the U.S. Of these 27 homicides, 22 were transgender women and feminine-presenting people of color,[2] illustrating the increased violence faced by those living at the intersections of gender- and race-related oppression. These statistics alone are reason enough to sound an immediate and sweeping call to action from teachers at all levels.

There is hope, though, and a great motivation for early childhood teachers to get right to work turning these statistics around. While 40% of all NCTE survey respondents had attempted suicide, family support (or lack thereof) made a significant difference. Of the respondents who reported having unsupportive families, 54% had attempted suicide, compared to only 37% of respondents with supportive families (James *et al.* p. 8). Similar numbers were found for those who had been bullied and harassed in school, compared to those who had not (p. 132). Early childhood teachers are uniquely positioned to directly impact both of these important factors. Given our close relationships with families that K–12 teachers do not have, we have a chance to prime all parents for supporting their children's gender health right from the start. We also have the opportunity to educate *all* children about gender diversity and introduce them to role models of a variety of genders (puppets and characters from books and stories make good role models in addition to real life adults). We have the responsibility to teach children to push back against rigid gender stereotypes. We want to teach this early in life, before they have formed hardened ideas about gender norms and those who break them. We want to direct their focus towards changing gender inequalitites, not changing their gender expansive peers.

Young children break gender stereotypes with an open heart, and often experience heartbreak when they are scolded or shamed for it by their peers or adults. We cannot "do no harm" without recognizing that harm is already being done. We believe that gender expansive children are not "at risk" until they experience external messaging that instills shame and self-doubt, and we feel it is the responsibility of early childhood teachers to take up the task of removing those risks from the paths of those open-hearted children.

What about *Free to Be You and Me* and the Feminist Movement? Working for gender inclusive early education is not a new idea, right? It is true that *Free to Be You and Me* (Thomas, 2013) and the feminist movement inspired dialogue and progress in supporting young children to have more choices about traditionally gendered activities and behaviors. It is now common for teachers actively to encourage young children not to be limited by strict gender roles and assumptions in their play and activities. Children are encouraged to wear whatever clothes they feel most comfortable wearing and to have freedom to play with the toys and games that interest them most. The legacy of this earlier gender inclusive movement was to disrupt such ideas as "Only girls can play with dolls and only boys can play with trucks," and "Only girls have long hair and boys can't wear pink."

Gender rules like these are often challenged in our current society—although girls are now provided with more options to wear traditional "boy" clothes or play with "boy" toys than the reverse. This is a result of many years of feminist protest and advocacy, but it is also related to the fact that femininity and femaleness are traditionally marginalized compared to masculinity and maleness. Young girls who want to play in the dirt and engage in rough-and-tumble activities are moving away from the devalued feminine. In contrast, young boys who want to care for dolls and wear sparkly tutus are sacrificing their privileged status as male and masculine to engage in femininity. These children are often bullied heavily and shamed for their gendered behaviors.

Many resources exist for activities and frameworks guiding teachers on how they can help break down traditional gender stereotypes (what girls are "supposed" to do or how boys are "supposed" to look). And yet, as Blaise and Taylor conclude in a 2012 research review in *Young Children*, these feminist efforts aren't working. They explain that such strategies as "providing books, posters, and other materials that present images of women and men engaged in roles or activities not traditionally associated with their gender and encouraging girls to play with blocks and boys to play with dolls…unfortunately…have not been particularly successful and, despite the long-term collective efforts of many teachers, children continue to reproduce gender stereotypes" (p. 89). These efforts are simply not enough.

Previous calls for gender equity did not extend children's agency (the ability to act independently and to participate in decisions that impact them) **beyond activities and behaviors and into the realm of gender identity.** In the 2010 edition of *Anti-Bias Education (ABE) for Young Children and Ourselves* (Derman-Sparks & Olsen Edwards, 2010), for example, it is made clear that children should be allowed to choose their toys, their clothes, and the ways they express themselves, but that teachers should "help preschoolers understand that being a girl or boy depends on how their bodies are made" (p. 94). Under this premise, a child is given no agency to determine and communicate about their gender-identity (what they know themselves to be inside) nor to explore gender identity options beyond the gender assigned to them at birth. This is the biggest difference between this book and previous books describing gender inclusive early childhood. Previous books, including ABE, have described the importance of challenging gender stereotypes. This goal is still very important, as strict gender roles are damaging for all children and adults. However, giving children agency over their identity communicates messages of welcome, acknowledgment, and respect to children who may feel at odds with the gender label assigned to them at birth.

Anti-Bias Education is currently being revised, and the 2020 edition will include a gender diversity framework that positions the child as agent of their own gender identity and expression. We recommend this forthcoming resource!

Most children are given no choice to declare their gender identity. Instead, a gender is assigned to them, usually based on their genitalia at birth, if not earlier (some children are born with "ambiguous genitalia" that confuses doctors — see "intersex" definition in Chapter 1. These children have historically been forced into a binary gender assignment as well.) Then this gender assignment is reinforced by everyone around them on a daily basis. If offered any kind of choice, they have two options: are you a boy or a girl? Children are constantly observing and listening to others in their daily interactions. What they see, hear, and observe related to gender significantly informs how they develop their awareness of who they are (their identity) and how they fit into their families and communities. As with every other aspect of child agency in early childhood education, our role as teachers is to create a space in which children can communicate their truths to us, and in which we can hear and honor them. Given the latest research on children's gender, we wrote this book to expand beyond previous calls for gender equity that were limited to children's behaviors and activities, to include agency over self-exploration and identity.

We believe it is essential that young children have the right and agency to tell us, the adults (parents, teachers, and others), what they understand their gender identities to be. Diane Ehrensaft, the director of mental health at the University of California San Francisco's Child and Adolescent Gender Center and a leading researcher and writer on gender expansive youth, wisely states, **"it is not for us to say, but for the children to tell"** (Ehrensaft, 2016). What she means by this statement is that adults cannot decide what a child's deeply felt sense of gender identity is. Only children know what is authentically true inside their hearts and minds, and only they can tell us what their true gender identities are. Creating an inclusive and welcoming environment where children feel safe enough to share what they feel inside is critical. This can make the difference between a child learning to feel accepted and developing a sense of belonging, or a child internalizing shame and self-doubt that can lead to serious consequences for their futures. Ehrensaft (2016a) reinforces this point. She states: "Parents, families and teachers have little control over their children's gender identity, but extensive influence over their children's gender health, gender expressions and feelings of affirmation."

Goal of this book

The goal of this book is to provide early childhood professionals working with infants, toddlers, preschoolers, and early elementary school-aged children with the knowledge and skills they need to create both gender justice in their classrooms and programs informed by the most contemporary understandings and research on gender. We want to **transform the way early childhood professionals understand young children's gender identities and gender development.** We want to expand the language and teaching practices used by early childhood teachers beyond the traditional binary of boy and girl to recognize gender as a deeply personal and diverse concept that children begin to explore and identify with as early as their toddler years.

Through many authentic vignettes and teacher-friendly strategies, everything in this book is written specifically for the early childhood field with a particular focus on the adults directly serving young children and their families. The information and strategies presented throughout this book are developmentally supportive and beneficial for ALL children, and they are **essential for gender expansive children** and their families. We want all early childhood teachers to have the skills and knowledge they need to support all children's gender health and to work responsively and effectively with children who do not fit neatly into the gender box (male or female) assigned to them at birth.

Throughout the book we use the word **"teacher"** to represent the diverse range of professionals who work with young children and their families. We understand that those who serve our youngest children use a range of other formal titles—e.g., provider, caregiver, care teacher, care provider, child care provider, teacher aide, instructional aide, family child care provider, and others. Our decision to refer to "teachers" throughout the book is only to provide a consistent term for readers. The content of the book applies to all adults who work directly with, or on behalf of, infants, toddlers, preschoolers, and early elementary-aged children.

What do we mean when we talk about gender justice in early childhood?

Gender justice in early childhood begins with a commitment to create inclusive environments that respect and acknowledge the authentic lived experiences and strengths of all children. Truly inclusive programs recognize that we live in a diverse society and that this diversity is valuable and should be visible, acknowledged, and respected. Inclusive programs are **strength-based**. A strength-based approach assumes that all children and families have resources, personal characteristics, and relationships that can be mobilized to enhance their learning, development, and well-being, no matter how many risk factors or challenges they face (Center for the Study of Social Policy, 2018).

Strength-based early childhood programs **value children's voices**. This is shown by integrating children's ideas, interests, feelings, desires, and perspectives into the program, and creating opportunities for children to authentically participate in decisions that impact their daily experiences. A strength-based approach rejects deficit thinking that places blame on children, families, cultural groups, or communities for children's poor educational or health outcomes rather than considering larger institutional and structural forms of oppression that inequitably hold children back (e.g., wealth inequality, racism).

Strength-based programs **reject pathologizing language**—language that makes assumptions that children who diverge from dominant cultural gender norms are deficient or sick, have something wrong with them, or need to be fixed or saved. Instead, inclusive programs communicate that gender, like other social categories (e.g., race, class, age, ability/disability), is complex and diverse—and this diversity should be acknowledged, respected, and celebrated.

At the foundation of inclusive early childhood programs are respectful, responsive, and attuned relationships between adults and children. Adults who form positive and attuned relationships with young children support them to develop the "emotional glue" they will need for all future relationships (Perry, 2013, p. 2). Attunement happens when an adult listens to a child so intently that the child learns that what they think and feel matters. They "feel felt" by the adult (Levine & Kline, 2007). The adult's interest in the child validates the child's presence and helps the child feel a sense of belonging, safety, and protection. **Attuned interactions become a foundation for children to develop a strong sense of self.**

It is through their earliest interactions with their parents/guardians, teachers, and caregivers that children learn to trust or distrust themselves and others. It is here that they discover whether their needs will be taken care of and to what extent the adults around them will provide physical and emotional security and protection. Loving and attuned adults who are responsive to children's needs can significantly reduce children's stress and can support them to develop resiliency and coping skills in the face of stress they do experience.

Inclusive early childhood programs treat families as partners in the education and care of young children. When families are recognized as partners, there is an understanding that parents and guardians are their children's first and most important teachers. Quality early childhood programs support teachers and program leaders to build respectful and strength-based partnerships with families. In a partnership, the assumption is that the teaching and learning will go both ways. As early childhood teachers, we have important knowledge and skills to share with parents and families. However, we have a tremendous amount to learn from them as well, to ensure that we are being respectful, and culturally and linguistically responsive in our communication and interactions. There are many ways to engage in responsive, strength-based relationships with families. Most importantly, we must express genuine interest in getting to know families and partnering with them to support their children. This begins by asking them about the goals and dreams they have for their children, any concerns they have, the forms of support they would like their children to receive, and what they want their children to learn while attending the early childhood program.

To extend this partnership with families to support our gender inclusive program, we must be prepared to have conversations with all families about supporting children's gender health. As you will learn throughout this book, gender is a rich and diverse aspect of each of our identities, but it is also heavily regulated by social norms and expectations. When a young child experiences this kind of regulation while they are trying to explore and discover where they fit in the world of gender, it can have serious negative consequences. Your partnerships with families should include the goal of understanding gender health and how it can be both supported and hindered, and striving together to support the gender health of all children. Creating gender inclusive environments takes everyone's participation: that's what *inclusive* means!

However, this book does not stop at inclusion. Creating gender inclusive environments is a necessary foundation, but it is not sufficient for achieving gender justice in early childhood. A focus on inclusion can be thought of as pro-diversity—inviting all voices to the table. **A focus on justice must also be anti-oppression—seeking out and disrupting the systems of power and oppression that benefit some people while hurting others.**

Creating gender justice starts with the relationships we build. When we create attuned, caring relationships with children, treat families as partners, and pay attention to the strengths of each, we are able to move past inclusion and begin the work of gender justice. A gender justice approach sees the damage caused to individuals and communities by compulsory and rigidly binary gender (see end of Chapter 1). It recognizes that this damage is intensified by both the power imbalance embedded in the gender binary that results in the devaluing of women and femininity, and the disrespect for labor that is coded female such as care work including early childhood education. A gender justice approach seeks to lessen this damage not only by healing the wounds but by changing the entire paradigm. There are many ways and many levels on which to do this work.

Anti-bias education (Derman-Sparks & Olsen Edwards, 2010) is an early childhood foundational approach grounded in research, and has four interlocking goals: identity, diversity, justice, and activism. The first goal, **identity**, is about supporting young children to develop a sense of pride in themselves and their families, including their social identities. In relation to gender, this requires the basic (yet radical) concept of **gender agency**: "I get to determine who I am, what my gender identity is, what I want to be called, and how I want to express myself, and whatever I determine is wonderful and valid—even if my answer is 'I don't know yet!'" However, a child's agency is limited by the paths they can imagine are available to them. See Chapter 4 for tips on how to integrate diverse gender narratives into your teaching.

The second goal, **diversity**, is about recognizing that everyone else's social identities, choices, lifestyles, and other differences are wonderful and valid—no more and no less than one's own. Part of this goal is about becoming comfortable talking about human differences. It requires adults to break the silence we often resort to in our attempt to avoid difficult conversations or offend someone. In relation to **gender diversity**, this goal can be expressed: "I will believe you when you tell me your gender identity. I will respect your agency and embodiment, and I will call you what you want to be called!" It also establishes in our school we expect you to respect other children's identities, however they name them.

The third goal of anti-bias education, **justice**, is about recognizing unjust or unfair actions and situations when they arise. This includes recognizing stereotypes (messages about a group of people that isn't true of everyone in the group—such as "Boys like sports"). It also includes recognizing when someone is being excluded on the basis of their social identity. This ranges from the blatant "No boys allowed!" to the more insidious "Boys line up here, girls line up there"—where TGE children are excluded by omission or forced to choose a side that might not fit. This goal also involves building children's awareness that unfairness hurts. To distinguish this piece from our overall gender justice framework, we call this goal **recognizing gender bias**. We also build on this goal to include recognizing unjust or unfair systems and assumptions built into our programs, laws, and cultures. This type of inequality is called **structural and institutional oppression** (Adams & Zuniga, 2016). Structural and institutional oppression allow harm to be done even without conscious bias or hate on an individual level.

The fourth goal is **activism**. This is about supporting children to become advocates for themselves and others, speaking up and acting in response to unfairness. This goal includes individual acts, such as telling a grown-up, "I want to be called 'she.' It hurts me when you call me 'he,'" or telling others, "That's not fair! You're excluding him." It also includes joining together with others to solve problems of structural or institutional unfairness or injustice. To share an example from *ABE* (Derman-Sparks & Olsen Edwards, 2010, p. 99), when one class saw a "Man wanted" sign while on a walk, they discussed it and wrote a letter to the shop owner about how it excluded people and why that wasn't fair. (The owner changed the sign to "Good worker wanted"!) When we engage children in processes like these, they learn that yes—injustice happens—but we have the power to do something about it. Individually and together, we can create change. We can become **gender advocates**.

A key tenet of anti-bias education (Derman-Sparks and Olsen Edwards, 2010) is that what we are doing with children also applies to our work with other adults and within ourselves. In this light, the **gender advocacy** goal about taking action is especially important.

These anti-bias education goals and the other aspects of gender justice that we have highlighted so far are small-scale, in the sense that they can happen within ourselves, and within our programs. However, it is crucial that we keep the larger picture in mind as we engage in this work. Particularly, we must think about how resources for creating gender justice are distributed to programs across race and class lines. Often, change starts from fierce parent advocates who are willing to take on a school administration to carve out a space for their child. But what happens when those parents are working two or three jobs and don't have time to take this on? What happens when a parent shows up to a support group for families of TGE children, and discovers they're the only person of color present? Or they can't come to the support group in the first place, because they don't speak English confidently enough to join, or because they're a single parent and the group doesn't offer childcare? What if you don't have the cash to buy this very book? Just as gender identity intersects with other identities on an individual level (see Intersectionality section in Chapter 1), so does gender justice intersect with other justice issues—economic justice and racial justice among others—on a systemic level.

While we don't have space in this book to explore it in depth, we do want you to think about this larger issue of access to gender diversity resources. If you are working within a well-resourced early childhood environment, consider how you can share your gender justice resources (including time and monetary resources) beyond the confines of that program. (Remember to act *with* communities with fewer resources, not *for* them. Relationships are key.)

If you are working within an under-resourced program, reflect on the strengths you already have within your program's community, and don't be afraid to pull on wider connections and state your program's needs. For example, one family care provider wanted to grow her library to include gender expansive literature and other diverse books, but she did not have the budget for it. She made a list of desired books and shared it on social media. By the end of that year, her library had doubled in size, and children in her program could find reflections of themselves on the bookshelf. This is a small step in the grand scheme of things but a huge one for those children in that time and place.

There are many barriers to doing gender justice work successfully— both external and internal. Building awareness about the challenges you may face is an important first step in learning how to prevent and/or effectively address them. While we will address many external barriers throughout this book (pushback from co-workers, administrators, and families, as well as structural barriers such as lack of resources), it is best to start by honestly recognizing potential barriers that are internal to you and your own process. The most significant internal barriers you might face include managing your fears, navigating discomfort in your learning process, and having the courage to address your biases.

Fear

Fear can be a normal experience when approaching new information (as can excitement – and they often go hand in hand!). This is especially true when learning new things about a subject—like gender—we might have thought we already understood pretty well. You may have fears associated with change as you are asked to learn new ideas about gender that begin with a process of unlearning things you were taught growing up. You might feel fearful of saying or doing the wrong thing, and this fear might be significant enough that it has, up to now, prevented you from saying or doing anything. Many teachers and parents we have talked to have expressed this type of fear, especially the first time they had a TGE child in their classroom (that they knew of) or when their own child expressed a transgender identity. You may want desperately to support that child, but a fear of "screwing it up" might have you frozen and feeling that the best or easiest strategy is not to engage with that child about gender at all. Other parents and teachers have expressed to us a fear of almost the opposite—they are worried they might be pushing children to think too much about gender. Still other teachers wonder what will happen if they support a child who expresses a gender other than the one they were assigned but then later they "change their mind" (a topic we will discuss throughout this book).

Our advice as you read this book—and as you work to strengthen gender justice in your early childhood programs—is to notice, honor, and be willing to explore all the fears that come up for you. You will be guided to discover your fears, to name them, to work to identify what is at the root of your fears (where your fears are coming from and what they mean to you), and how your fears are potentially impacting your work with children. **And, at the end of the day, we encourage you to err on the side of trusting that children know who they are even if it might feel scary for you.** As adults who are often seeking concrete answers to big questions, we must be careful not to project our fears and discomforts onto the children we work with, but rather, to be brave in following their leads into a more expansive and creative world of gender where every child gets to make the rules about who they are and how they express themselves.

Discomfort

If you have picked up this book, it is probably because you have a desire to support and protect all the children in your care. Reading through this book, you will be asked to reflect on the ways you are supporting or discouraging gender justice. Reflecting on your practices, thinking about gender in new and exploratory ways with children, reshaping your environment to encourage gender creativity, and exploring other ideas presented in this book might make you uncomfortable, especially if you are just getting started on your journey. You may discover that something you have done for years could be harmful to certain children and this could evoke discomfort and a range of feelings including defensiveness, anger, embarrassment, shame, disbelief, and confusion. There is also the possibility you will feel supported and eager! We invite you to explore all of your feelings courageously. If you are struggling, remind yourself: the only way we can see deep and systemic changes that will make this world safer for TGE people to thrive is if we accept that **feeling uncomfortable is part of an authentic learning process.**

Bias

We all have biases. Biases are woven into the fabric of our laws, policies, organizations, cultural practices, the stories we tell, and the stereotypes that persist in our societies. Every individual person is affected by bias in countless ways on a daily basis, and these can be both conscious and unconscious. Individuals can be conscious of their behaviors (requesting that children line up as boys and girls), yet not realize that they are based on unconscious attitudes (e.g., belief in gender as a binary). Additionally, individuals may be conscious of an attitude they have (e.g., "Girls should not study to be engineers") without understanding its roots in an unconscious stereotype (e.g., "Only boys are good at math"). The attitudes that influence biases are often based in stereotypes about a group of people rooted on partial information, misinformation, or missing information (Adams & Zuniga, 2016). By overgeneralizing, stereotypes mask the diversity that exists among individuals. Although individuals, groups, and institutions often deny that their attitudes and behaviors are intended to discriminate against anyone, research establishes that our biases do cause harm to marginalized and excluded individuals and groups. Transgender and gender expansive individuals are continually marginalized by policies that assume that everyone fits into two gender boxes.

Oppression

Attitudes and behaviors that are based in stereotypes can contribute to **oppression**. Oppression is the systematic and prolonged mistreatment of a group of people within a country or society. It is characterized by an uneven distribution or use of power between groups where one group is privileged (e.g., people who identify with and are read by the others as the gender they were assigned at birth and men/masculine people) and engages in manipulation and control over the other group(s) (e.g., TGE individuals and women/feminine people) regardless of whether this use of power is conscious or intentional.

> Oppression is the systematic and prolonged mistreatment of a group of people. It is built into our daily lives.
>
> Oppression extends beyond the actions of individuals. It shapes the systems we live and work in and the structures in society (e.g., education, health care, housing).
>
> Oppression exists within institutions and organizations at every level (e.g., harmful or inequitable policies, practices, interactions, and behaviors).
>
> Oppression impacts learning, teaching, leading, and decision-making.
>
> Addressing oppression and bias triggers strong emotions.
>
> Systemic oppression is the source of a lot of trauma in our society and impacts every aspect of children's lives whether they are advantaged or disadvantaged as a result of its existence.
>
> We all need to heal from the effects of oppression.
>
> National Equity Project, Oakland, California
> (www.nationalequityproject.org)

Beverly Tatum has described the impact of prejudice and oppression using the metaphor of "smog" to discuss racism in society. Her description of an oppressive smog that is everywhere around us and causing harm on a daily basis is a metaphor that can be used to describe gender oppression as well. Tatum explains:

> *Prejudice is one of the inescapable consequences of living in a racist society. Cultural racism—the cultural images and messages that affirm the assumed superiority of Whites and the assumed inferiority of people of color—is like smog in the air. Sometimes it is so thick it is visible, other times it is less apparent, but always, day in and day out, we are breathing it in. None of us introduce ourselves as "smog-breathers" (and most of us don't want to be described as prejudiced), but if we live in a smoggy place, how can we avoid breathing the air? (Tatum, 1997, pp. 5–6)*

While we don't assume anyone reading this book believes strongly that boys shouldn't play with dolls or girls shouldn't play in rough-and-tumble games, we also know that we all have biases based on deeply held assumptions in society about gender. **It is impossible to grow up surrounded by the "gender binary" smog, without being deeply affected in ways that consciously and unconsciously influence our attitudes and actions.** We have to be honest with ourselves that we each have biases about gender, often based in stereotypes, which hurt children and especially TGE children. Without acknowledging this truth from the beginning, early childhood teachers will struggle to make progress in creating gender justice in programs for young children.

Stepping outside Your comfort zone

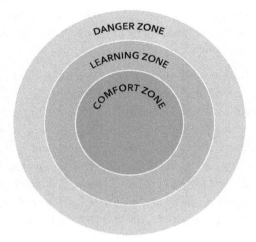

Comfort zones: A model that is widespread in adventure and outdoor education theory. Adapted from Panicucci (2007).

The comfort zone model, which has been used in adventure education for many years, can help us to address fear, discomfort, and the risks of uncovering our own biases, and to think about where we should be aiming as we go through this work. The model shown here is one of many variations on a concept introduced by Luckner and Nadler in their 1997 book, *Processing the Experience: Strategies to Enhance and Generalize Learning*. They proposed the idea that most of us spend our days engaged in activities and interactions that are relatively comfortable for us, but that deep learning and introspection doesn't happen much in this space. To truly learn and grow, we must venture to the edge of our **comfort zones** into what is shown here as the **learning zone**. In this zone, we are inherently uncomfortable—engaging in new and unfamiliar experiences, interactions, and thought practices. We find ourselves less skilled and less competent than we are if we stay where we're comfortable. In the learning zone we stumble, struggle, grapple, fail, flail, and fall, but we are learning quickly as we do so. Beyond the learning zone, as we get increasingly less comfortable with our circumstances, is the **danger zone**. In this space, we tend to stop learning because our fears, discomfort, and anxiety are strong enough that we panic rather than focus on learning.

We want you to aim for the learning zone while you read this book and engage in this transformative work. If you find you are sitting in the comfort zone, not feeling challenged or uncomfortable at all, we encourage you to dig deeper. Even the transgender members of this author team know firsthand that we will always have biases to uncover, assumptions to rattle, and new perspectives to explore. On the other hand, if you start to feel overwhelmed, confused, defensive, dismissive, or otherwise disengaged with what you're reading, we suggest that you slow down. You may have reached your danger zone, in which we enter into a mindset of self-preservation similar to when we are in physical danger. In this case, though, it is our mind seeking to protect us from information that is threatening the beliefs we rely on for a stable worldview and sense of self.

For many people, gender is such a deeply ingrained belief system that even just getting through the glossary in this book will be mentally exhausting and might elicit strong emotional responses. Take time to digest the information you're learning. Talk with a friend who is doing this work too. We will provide many contextual examples, but we encourage you to seek out even more stories and narratives that illustrate the concepts you're having trouble grasping. If you read something that conflicts with your life experience or worldview, look for a blog, book, or video by someone for whom it might ring true. Practice imagining experiences you have never had and extending empathy beyond the things you understand through personal experience. Implement action steps one at a time. Go at the pace that works for you. When you experience the kind of extreme discomfort that gets in the way of learning, back up to where you are comfortable again and reflect on what it was that pushed you over the line into the danger zone. What are the underlying beliefs that were challenged? How can you reenter the work carefully, so as to stay in the learning zone?

Most importantly, get in the habit of noticing which zone you are in at any given point in your gender justice journey. Pay attention to your body and your physical responses to new ideas. When you get too comfortable, remember to push yourself. When you get too close to the danger zone, remember to slow down. Luckner and Nadler called this process **edgework**, where we consciously bring ourselves to the edges of what we are comfortable with but turn back before we panic—producing the deepest learning we can achieve. Once you get the hang of it, this discomfort becomes exciting, and we feel certain you will love your learning zone as much as we love ours!

Education is a healing practice and it's about justice and it's about our bodies. We have such possibility with children because of the flexibility of little kids, and because of the teaching force in early childhood. Teachers actually understand what transformation looks like. They have a different understanding of what's possible.
–Kate, Early Childhood Equity Trainer

Organization of the book

- **Chapter 1: Gender 101** introduces gender vocabulary, changing Western models of gender over time, gender myths, and children's developmental milestones related to gender in the early childhood years.

- **Chapter 2: Attuned and Responsive Relationships** introduces the importance of attunement and the relational supports that all children, but especially transgender and gender expansive (TGE) children, need in order to feel a sense of safety, belonging, and care so they can learn and thrive in early childhood classrooms. The consequences of not working for gender justice in early childhood environments are discussed.

- **Chapter 3: Strengthening Self-Awareness to Check Assumptions and Interrupt Biases about Gender** presents a reflection framework that teachers can use to strengthen awareness of the assumptions, beliefs, and biases they have in relation to children's gender. Several strategies are introduced that teachers can use to address their biases and to interrupt practices that send harmful messages to young children about gender.

- **Chapter 4: Co-Creating Dynamic Gender Justice Curricula and Early Childhood Environments** provides teachers with tangible ideas and a wide range of strategies they can use on a daily basis to create gender justice in their programs. Teachers learn about the importance of language choices, the role of children's play in supporting children's gender health, and how they can effectively respond when they observe gender bias and gender-related exclusion in their classroom.

- **Chapter 5: Gender Justice in Children's Literature** provides criteria teachers can use to identify quality children's literature that represents gender diversity in characters and storylines. Teachers also learn about the types of books and narratives to avoid when guiding children to learn about gender.

- **Chapter 6: Working with Families and Colleagues to Support Children's Gender Health and Create Gender Justice in Our Programs** includes tips for talking with families about TGE children, how to respond when families are resistant or uncomfortable with a gender diversity approach, and strategies for working with other teachers and administrators to **strengthen gender justice across a program.**

- **The final sections of the book include a conclusion, references, and a list of resources** readers will find useful for learning more about gender diversity.

Origin of anecdotes

This book includes many authentic vignettes drawn from conversations with young children and their families, TGE adults, and a range of early childhood teachers, advocates, and others working to serve children birth to five years of age. A range of firsthand stories provide opportunities for readers to increase their awareness, understanding, and empathy for the importance of creating gender justice in early childhood environments. These stories also help demonstrate the harm done to all children—but most especially gender expansive children and families—when this is not done. We are grateful for the generosity and kindness of all the individuals who shared their experiences with us for this book.

A note on pronouns and presumptions

Throughout this book, we refer to individuals with the last set of pronouns we are aware of them using. Current most respectful practice is to use a person's current pronoun even when talking about them in the past, at a time they did not use that pronoun. We use the singular "they" when we don't know an individual's pronouns or someone has indicated that they use "they/them" pronouns. The exception to this is Lucien, whose pronouns will flow through this book as we follow their journey.

When we describe genders as "presumed" or "presumed for now"—
such as: "Kayla, a (presumed-for-now) girl, loves Barbies and especially
loves adorning them with tattoos and mohawks"—we are indicating that
Kayla may not have verbally confirmed the adults' assignment that she is
a girl, but so far appears comfortable with that assignment and has not yet
contradicted it. We have chosen this language because we understand that
until there is a major societal shift, children will continue to be assigned
a gender at birth. While we are trying to move away from assuming,
presuming is subtly different. To **presume** is to "suppose to be the case on
the basis of probability," while to **assume** is to "suppose to be the case
without proof."[3] As we have mentioned, supporting children's gender
health requires a thorough reflection on the assumptions we make about
children, and a shift towards observations whenever possible. Presuming
is still not ideal, but it leaves room for shifting your assessment based
on tangible observations. As you get to know each child, and you create
spaces where they can safely communicate their gender(s) to you, you
will be able to shed even these presumptions in favor of authenticity and
agency for each individual child.

The gender justice self-study and classroom audit tool

At the end of each chapter, we will include a set of reflection questions
and prompts about specific aspects of your program and practice for you
to consider from a gender justice perspective. This tool is not meant to
be a simple checklist, which, once complete, will signal the end of one's
work towards gender justice. Rather, it is a way to identify areas where
you might want to focus your attention, a structure for you to create
a concrete plan towards change, and a jumping point for your lifelong
learning about gender justice and other forms of justice in your program.
Use this tool to identify where you and your program are now, where
you can make immediate change, and where you want to direct your
long-term energy.

Depending on your individual circumstances, you may decide
that there are some areas you have little to no control over. Maybe you
have an administrator who is adamantly against this work, or perhaps
your program can't afford new books and materials. We recommend
starting your work on the parts of the audit where you have the most
influence and can impact children most directly, but we also encourage

you to be creative in thinking about the areas where you foresee a significant roadblock. What strengths and resources can you leverage? If a direct route seems difficult, are there ways around the barrier? Or perhaps your program is very excited about this work and has lots of resources to make it a reality. How can you share those resources and your impact with programs that have greater barriers to justice?

For a printable version of this audit tool, including rich examples and room to map out your own action plan, please visit our website: www.genderjusticeinearlychildhood.com

"Since I'm No Gender": Text reads: "Since I'm a no-gender person I will go in the boys' restroom." The illustrator, 8½, explains that if you aren't a boy or a girl you still need to pick which bathroom to use, and suggests using the bathroom that is closer. Credit line: Chicken.

— Chapter 1 —

Gender 101

Gender vocabulary

To put it simply, I feel like a girl trapped in a boy's body, and I've felt that way ever since I was four. I never knew there was a word for that feeling, nor was it possible for a boy to become a girl, so I never told anyone and I just continued to do traditionally "boyish" things to try to fit in. When I was 14, I learned what transgender meant and cried of happiness. After ten years of confusion I finally understood who I was. (Alcorn, 2014)

One of the first steps early childhood teachers can take to create gender justice is to learn some shared vocabulary. Language is a powerful tool in understanding the world and ourselves, and early childhood is when both language and identity development are in overdrive. If children don't see themselves in the words they are given, they may make up words to reflect their identities, or they may struggle to understand where they fit in the world without words to describe their experiences.

These terms and their definitions will help you discuss gender accurately and openly with children, families, and your colleagues. As you review all this new vocabulary, you might worry that you won't remember all these terms or that you might make a mistake and say the wrong thing. These fears are normal! Most people share these worries when they are just learning about gender diversity. Try to be forgiving with yourself as you learn. You will make some mistakes and that is okay. The important thing is that you are taking the initiative to learn about gender. Everything you learn will help you become more aware, more responsive, and more inclusive for the young children in your care.

Talking about gender vocabulary: Learning to use gender vocabulary helps teachers discuss gender accurately and openly with children, families, and other adults. Credit line: Jonathan Julian.

We have put a lot of thought and care into choosing language that is empowering and promotes justice for young children and which is embraced by much of the TGE community. That said, we want to acknowledge that language is always evolving, and very quickly in this field. Also, language and labels can be highly personal. Not all terms are embraced by all gender expansive individuals (including "gender expansive"!). Some phrases that we use as umbrella terms other folks might define more narrowly, and vice versa. We recommend keeping an open mind as language evolves, and seeking terms that feel empowering to the children you work with in your communities. All children and adults should have agency over the language used to describe them.

The following are terms we believe will give all early childhood teachers a solid foundation to start talking about gender diversity.

Gender binary

This is the idea that there are only two genders—male and female—and that these neatly correspond to a person's anatomy and physiology and determine their personal preferences, styles, behavior, roles, and capabilities. It is important to note that this binary is not neutral. Within the context of a patriarchal culture, all things male and masculine are valued over all things female and feminine. While binary gender paints itself as natural and universal, like any cultural norm it is specific to a time and place. Many people are surprised to learn that one hundred years ago in the United States, pink was considered a boy's color and blue was for girls! While binary gender is the dominant gender concept among many cultures throughout the world, it is not universal.

Teachers may describe the gender binary to children by saying:

- "Some people think that there are only two genders and you can't choose. But we know that there are many genders!"

- "Some people say that girls have to be a certain way and boys have to be a certain way. These people might not know about other genders. They are still learning."

Many cultures acknowledge three or more genders

While Western society has held a binary view of gender and anatomy for quite some time, many cultures across the world and throughout history have acknowledged three or more genders. Every society has a version of male/masculine and female/feminine, but the other gender identities and roles in various cultures differ greatly. Some are highly regarded as spiritually unique individuals in their cultures, while others are shunned and treated as second-class citizens. These categories have arisen from the recognition of both anatomical variety and social variety when individuals do not fit neatly into the cultural expectations of male/masculine or female/feminine.

One of the most well-known third genders are the **hijras**[4] of the Indian subcontinent, who have legal recognition in some countries but not always equal rights under the law. Most hijras are assigned male at birth. While many of the indigenous cultures of this region once held hijras as an important cultural group with traditional roles in religion, British colonial influence put a social stigma on hijras, marking them as "immoral and corrupt" in the 1871 Criminal Tribes Act.[5] To this day, many hijras live in poverty and face extreme discrimination. Similarly, in the pre-colonial history of Hawai'i, **Māhū** were notable priests and healers taking on the roles of goddesses in traditional hula dances and other specific roles in society. **Māhū** were people with masculine and feminine traits, and considered to occupy a space "in the middle" or between kāne (male) and wāhine (female). They were highly revered until missionaries and colonizers brought stigma and discrimination. It is important to note that, in many regions of the world, Western cultural influences were what stigmatized or erased from view the indigenous gender groups.

Countless other cultures throughout history have had their own third (or more!) gender categories. From the many variations on **two-spirit** found in the different indigenous tribes of the Americas to the **fa'afafine** of Polynesia, from the **burrnesha** (sworn virgins) of Albania, to **muxe** of Latin America, and from androgynos of old Israel to Japanese **X-gender**, we see that the gender binary is far from universal!

Anatomy (structure of body parts) and physiology (functions and relationship of body parts)

All children have body parts and structures such as genitals, chromosomes, hormones, and genes, influencing how their bodies will grow and function. In a binary gender system, everyone is assigned to one of two categories (male or female) based on a simple visual inspection of external genitalia at birth or from an ultrasound before birth. However, biology is much more varied than those two categories would have you believe. Many people's bodies do not conform to this binary system, and are pathologized by medical and social systems that rely on it (see our definition of intersex, below). Furthermore throughout history and cultures, the medical definitions of male and female have changed many times as human anatomy was further studied. A distinction that was once only about genitals grew to consider gonads, chromosomes, and individual hormone levels—with increasing complexity and diversity discovered at each new level. Professionals still disagree about where exactly to draw a single line in the sand (Fausto-Sterling, 2000). The reality is that having only two labels to describe all our different bodies is a cultural choice, and one that does not adequately reflect the beauty that is our natural diversity.

In many discussions of gender, people make a distinction between bodies and identities by using the terms sex and gender respectively. A child's initial medical designation might be referred to as sex, biological sex, natal sex, or sex assigned at birth. Unfortunately, these terms are often used to overemphasize a false binary understanding of bodies and to minimize the importance and legitimacy of gender identity. An example is when someone refers to a transgender man as being "biologically female," and thus invalidating or minimizing his self-identification as male. It is important to use vocabulary that allows us to talk about bodies but also acknowledges biological diversity and respects the right of children and adults to determine their own authentic gender and name their own bodies ("I identify as male, and therefore my body is 'biologically male,' ovaries and all!"). We want to communicate that a person's body does not determine their gender—they do.

For these reasons, we use **anatomy and physiology** rather than sex to refer to bodies, and we consider **gender** to be a very large umbrella term that encompasses bodies, identities, and a lot more.

Young children might talk about their anatomy and physiology by saying:

- "My body has _____ [a penis, a vulva, a vagina, a scrotum]."
- "We all have _____ [genitals, a crotch, private parts, underwear parts]."

Teachers might talk about anatomy and physiology by saying:

- "We all have genitals, and each person's genitals look a little different from everyone else's. Vulvas, penises, and scrotums come in different sizes and shapes."
- "Many boys have penises, but some boys have vulvas and vaginas. Many girls have vulvas and vaginas, but some girls have penises."
- "Yes, you have what I would usually call a vulva. Do you use another word for it?"
- "Are you comfortable with me calling this a penis? Okay. Aim your penis into the toilet!"

Intersex

Intersex children are born with anatomy and physiology that do not fall easily into discrete binary medical categories of male or female whether due to ambiguous genitalia, chromosomal variations, hormone levels or sensitivities, or other factors (http://www.isna.org/faq/frequency). Intersex people make up about 2% of the population – about the same percentage as left-handed people, and redheads.[6] This significant percentage of the population has largerly remained invisible due to social stigma. In many countries, including the U.S., intersex children have historically been forced into one medical box or the other at birth. For children born with visibly ambiguous genitalia, this might be done through unnecessary genital surgeries in infancy. While these surgeries may ease parents' worries about their children to have a "normal" life, they do so at the expense of inflicting "irreversible physical and psychological harm" throughout the child's life. Many medical communities are changing their practices based on recommendations from adult intersex activists and their allies.[7]

Think it's all about XX or XY? Think again!

Most people know the two most common variations of sex chromosomes: XX for females and XY for males. But did you know that there are other known variations that children and adults might have?

X–Roughly 1 in 2,700 births (Turner syndrome)

XXX–Roughly 1 in 1,000 births

XXY–Roughly 1 in 500 designated male births (Klienfelter syndrome)

XYY–Roughly 1 in 1,000 designated male births (Jacob's or XYY syndrome)

(Zayed, nd)

In total, around 1 in every 1,700 children born is neither XX nor XY.[8] Many of them won't know they are intersex until puberty, and some go their whole lives without knowing!

Legal designation

Following close on the heels of medical designations of male and female are the legal designations that go with them. In most countries, a doctor's simple inspection of an infant's (or fetus's) externally visible genitalia results in not just a binary medical label but a legal designation that has a far-reaching impact on a person's life. In some places in the world, that legal designation determines whether a person can vote, own property, drive, or be granted any number of other government-regulated rights. The process of changing someone's legal designation after infancy varies state to state and country to country. There are some places where it is impossible to change one's legal designation from the one assigned at birth. Many transgender adults in the U.S. find themselves with a range of different legal gender designations between state-issued IDs, passports, birth certificates, medical records, and other documents based on whether changes are possible and accessible for each.

In this book, we use **legal designation** rather than sex when talking about the marker required for various types of paperwork. As discussed above, children's anatomy is not at all binary, but in most places legal designations still are. Using this term puts a degree of separation between a child who may not agree with their legal designation, and the designation itself. It also does better at capturing an individual's agency (or lack thereof) in being able to change their legal designation later in their lives if they wish. If someone wants to change their legal designation but can't (due to financial, legislative, or other barriers) the "problem" is structural or institutional, rather than being internal to that person. Not having access to a legal designation that matches one's identity is an example of structural and institutional oppression—where the gender binary is built into the legal system.

Teachers can talk about legal designation by saying:

- "Your paperwork says male, but only you know who you are."

- "When you were born, the doctors and other grown-ups guessed you were a girl, but you get to tell us if they were right or not."

Gender identity

This is one's deeply held sense of self as it relates to the world of gender. A person's gender identity is informed by the world around them— their culture, family, relationships, place in history, and more—but it is determined internally for each individual. Most children become conscious of their gender identity/ies between 18 and 30 months old (Halim, Bryant, & Zucker 2016). Some children develop a gender identity that matches their original legal designation (see cisgender) and some children develop a gender identity that is different from their original legal designation (see transgender/trans). Gender identity may be **fixed** (staying the same throughout one's life) or it may be **fluid** (changing over time and/or across contexts).

Gender identities—choice vs. agency

There is some disagreement in gender expansive communities over the use of the word **identity** to refer to one's gender. In many contexts, a term that was originally meant to convey agency has been used by those who disagree with the breaking down of gender barriers to imply that TGE individuals are simply making a choice not to follow the path that is expected of them (e.g., "Sure, you identify as a girl, but you're really a boy"). This debate about choice is a familiar theme in discussions of sexual orientation as well. Activists and advocates for LGBQ rights have worked for years to dispel the myth that being gay or lesbian or otherwise not heterosexual is a choice. The same is true for gender—TGE individuals do not simply choose to feel the way they feel inside or to be a gender other than the one assigned to them at birth.

Many other aspects of these individuals' lives are choices. Children will choose whether or not they will tell you about how they feel inside. They will choose whether or not they will express their gender freely. These choices will be made based on how safe they perceive their environment to be.

When we use the term **identity**, we want to be clear that we are not implying that a child chooses to be a certain gender. We are granting each child agency over identifying or naming their own gender(s), rather than being forced to accept the labels and designations placed on them by others.

We respect and support the decision by many TGE individuals to abandon the word **identity** in favor of just saying **gender**. In the context of this book, we ask readers to see the word "identity" as an embodiment of agency.

Cisgender

This term refers to individuals whose gender identity is the same as their legal designation at birth. Most people can be described as cisgender men and women. The term was derived from the Latin preposition *cis* meaning "on this side" (https://www.etymonline.com/word/cis-; https://www.merriam-webster.com/dictionary/cis). While this is a relatively new term, and a word that is unknown to many of the people it describes, its importance is often understated. In most societies, cisgender experiences are considered normal while everyone else is seen as other. By including the word cisgender in our vocabulary, it is possible to name this power dynamic and begin to disrupt the societal norms that lead TGE individuals to be marginalized (i.e., regarded as invisible, or seen as insignificant or as outliers). For example, without the prefix cis-, cismen are just men while transmen can never fully attain that label. Without the prefix cis-, cisgender people are often thought of as real or normal men and women, while transgender people are thought of as somehow less than real or as abnormal (they are pathologized). While cisgender people and experiences are more common, they are no more real or normal than transgender people and gender expansive experiences.

Young children might talk about cisgender identity by saying:

- "When I was born, the doctor thought I was a boy, and I think I'm a boy too."

- "When I was born, grown-ups guessed I was a girl and I'm still a girl."

Transgender or trans

These are individuals whose gender identity is different from their legal gender designation at birth in any way. We use these two terms interchangeably, but not everyone in TGE communities agrees that they are interchangeable. We use transgender and trans as umbrella terms to include individuals who identify outside the male/female gender binary, including people who identify as both male and female, as neither, or as any number of other genders. Some folks define one of the two terms more narrowly and the other as a broader umbrella, but we do not make that distinction.

TGE identities: teens and adults

It can be hard for people to envision genders outside the gender binary. Following are a few of the many terms that adolescent and adult communities have embraced as identities, and some loose definitions of how they are used.

Gender fluid. Individuals who defy the norms of binary gender and either slide along a gender spectrum or weave their own intricate individual patterns of gender. The word "fluid" refers to the potential for individuals to move through and explore and/or identify with different genders day to day and throughout their lives.

Genderqueer. A term that represents a gender identity and a social movement among youth and adults who question and challenge traditional beliefs about gender. They are striving for new, more expansive, diverse, and inclusive understandings about gender that liberate individuals from the constraints of the gender binary.

Agender. Similar to genderqueer, individuals who identify as agender are breaking down traditional beliefs about gender as a binary. Gender individuals may identify as having a gender but not a specific gender or they may not identify with having a gender at all.

Nonbinary. While we are under the transgender/trans heading in this glossary, nonbinary is often considered more of a separate circle on the Venn diagram of gender, overlapping with transgender and trans (identities don't like being boxed in neatly!). Nonbinary identities are broadly defined as any identities that defy the social pressure to choose one and only one—male or female. Kylie identifies as male and female, but also includes gender educator and gender troublemaker as part of his identity! Nonbinary is sometimes called "**enby**" from the abbreviation, nb.

Trans woman/Trans man/Trans girl/Trans boy. These are often the labels used by transgender individuals who identify with one of the binary categories of male or female, but not with the one designated to them at birth. Some people condense the phrase into a single word (eg. transwoman, transman). For others, it is important to keep a space in the label—trans woman or trans man—to indicate that trans describes a kind of woman or man but that their femaleness/maleness is valid and unqualified in and of itself.

NOTE: One individual may have several identities and use many terms for themself!

TGE identities: young children

While some young children may use a term like nonbinary if they have heard it in their community, it is more common for children to come up with their own words or use more simple or concrete language. Here are a few examples of terms that children have organically used for themselves to describe genders outside of (or more inclusive than) simply girl or boy.

Boy-girl/Girl-boy. Meaning both boy and girl.

Everything. When young children become aware of multiple gender options, they sometimes opt for "all of the above"—intuitively grasping a concept that many adults struggle with.

Kid. "Why are you asking if I'm a boy or a girl? I'm just a kid!"; "We're all kids!"

Just call me by my name. Some children won't want to be called a boy or a girl: they'll say "Just call me Cienna!"

Gender smoothie. One of Ehrensaft's patients told her "You take everything about gender, throw it in a blender, press the button, and you've got me" (Ehrensaft, 2016b, p. 40).

Gender prius. A play on the hybrid car, this describes a child who considers themself half-boy and half-girl (Ehrensaft, 2016b, p. 36).

What terms have you heard children come up with to describe their genders? Would you hear those children differently now than you did in the past?

Hemin, Age 5

"In-betweener": In one preschool classroom, the children were working together at group time over several weeks to write a song-book about the classroom community. One child was inspired to create this illustration of an in-betweener for the song-book after a discussion about gender identity. Credit line: Tink Hemin.

Gender expression

These are the ways in which people externally communicate their gender to others through behavior, clothing, hairstyle, voice (pitch, intonation, volume), activities, or mannerisms and ways of moving that their culture associates with masculinity, femininity, or androgyny (a combination of or ambiguity between masculine and feminine). For example, in contemporary Western cultures, long hair, dresses, playing with dolls, and the color pink are often associated with femininity/femaleness whereas short hair, pants, rough-and-tumble play, and the color blue with masculinity/maleness.

A child's gender expression may or may not align with cultural norms and expectations based on either their legal designation or their gender identity. For example, a child who is designated male at birth but identifies as female may still express herself as a "tomboy" who likes to play in the dirt and has short hair. Many children will explore different gender expressions to see what feels right for them. As TGE children grow up and live authentically in their gender identities, some will choose new names and/or pronouns, some will choose to take hormones or have surgery, and some will choose not to do any of those things as part of their gender expressions.

The clothes that parents and caregivers provide for their children, the haircuts they are given, and many other aspects of gender expression are often decided without much input from the children themselves. Some children are not allowed to express themselves in the ways they want to, and are instead forced into gender expressions that are not authentic.

Young children's gender expression is reflected in such statements as:

- "I like to wear _____."
- "My favorite toys and games are _____."

Young children might talk about TGE expression by saying:

- "I am a girl, but I like all the boy things."
- "I am a boy fairy princess."

Here is how eight-year-old Alex, a TGE child, described his gender expression in kindergarten:

I felt a little embarrassed [to wear dresses]. I didn't wear dresses a lot because they [classmates] might laugh at me. Actually, it doesn't matter cause they didn't laugh at me... Just 'cause you wear a dress doesn't mean someone is able to be like, "Haha! You're wearing a pink dress. I'm not going to play with you"... Just because they have a certain gender...it doesn't mean you can't play. Because actually there's no such thing as girl colors and boy colors and girl clothes and boy clothes.

Pronouns

We use pronouns every day in almost every statement we make to refer to people. Familiar pronouns reinforce a gender binary (he/him and she/her). These pronouns are authentic for some people, but many transgender/gender expansive individuals use gender-neutral pronouns (singular they/them or alternative terms such as ze/hir or others). Referring to an individual, including a child, by the pronoun they identify with communicates an important message of respect: "I acknowledge and respect your authentic gender identity and welcome you being your authentic gender self." Using accurate pronouns is a critically important action that teachers and adults can take to support TGE children.

Adults cannot determine what pronouns are most authentic to a child just by looking at them. The easiest way to find out is to create a culture where children are asked and invited to name their pronouns. Adults can model this practice by including their own pronouns when they introduce themselves to others. This communicates to children that they are safe and can be their authentic selves when they are in your program. This also teaches children that they have agency over the language that others use to talk about them. Young children may explore the use of different pronouns in their play, art, or throughout conversations with their peers and teachers. Learning to ask about individuals' pronouns can be difficult at first for adults, but with practice, it will become much easier. Young children can learn from their earliest years to ask about others' pronouns. By being intentional about respecting children's pronouns, early childhood teachers create a more just culture that respects and welcomes children of all genders.

Young children might use different pronouns as they explore their gender identities:

- "I want to be called 'he.'"

- "I want to be called 'he' and 'she'!"

- "I'm a 'she' in this game."

- "I'm a boy today. Call me 'he'!"

- "I don't want to be called 'she' anymore. Can I be called 'he' again?"

- "I want to be called 'they.'"

- "Just call me Cienna!"

Gender expansive(ness)

Gender expansive (also gender creative) refers to anyone who is exploring, expressing, and identifying their genders in ways that challenge cultural norms and expand our binary understanding of gender. Gender expansive is a broad umbrella term that includes children who (one day or already) identify as transgender people, as well as children who (one day or already) identify as cisgender people but whose gender expression is not confined to binary expectations of their gender. Gender expansiveness, as a concept, allows children to push the boundaries of what we think we know about gender through creativity and imagination. Even the word "expansive" gives rise to an ever-growing number of possible combinations of identities, expressions, and bodies—making way for smoothies, priuses, boy-girls, girl-boys, in-betweeners, and every new gender that children have yet to declare (see box above). This is followed by the hope that the laws and institutions in which we must all live as gendered beings will grow and expand along with us.

Young children might talk about being gender expansive by saying:

- "I am a girl, but I like all the boy things."

- "This is a boy's dress."

- "Girls can have beards too, because my mom has a beard!"

Social transition

As some children explore their identities, expressions, and the language they want used to describe them (names, pronouns, etc.), they might let the adults in their lives know that they would like to change some of the aspects of their gender that were assigned to them by others. Of course, they must be given a loving and supportive environment, and agency over those decisions, before they are likely to express these needs openly. When a child wants the people around them to change how they interact with them—new name, pronouns, identity, etc.—we call the process of adopting those changes a social transition. Some children and families choose to move their child to a new school or program: to start fresh with new friends using their new name and pronouns right from the start. Other children might want to have a slow and subtle transition at school, by telling their closest friends first and then proceeding as they feel comfortable. Still others might want to shout it from the rooftops and celebrate with cake. We know one third grader who, with his mom's help, put together a PowerPoint presentation to teach the whole class about gender and his new name and pronouns! A social transition should follow the child's lead, and the child and family should be involved in every step and every decision. Nothing should be done without the child's consent and agency.

Assumptions vs. observations

One important theme to notice about the terms we are introducing is that they move us away from making assumptions about children and towards making observations together with children. For example, the term "sex" makes assumptions about a child's body, while talking about anatomy and physiology is based on what we observe about bodies. The terms and concepts we've presented about gender—identity, expression, pronouns, etc.—are grounded in observing and listening to the children themselves. Changing our language changes the way we think about gender and shifts agency from doctors, politicians, and other adults into the hands of the children whose lives are affected by these assumptions.

Well, some people guess what genders are but it's better if you just-maybe you should just ask if you're uncertain. The best way is to ask. -Angus, 6 years

Gender attribution

This is the process by which an individual decides what gender they believe a child to be by making assumptions from their gender expression (e.g., clothing, hairstyle, voice) and visible aspects of their anatomy and physiology (e.g., body shape). Gender attribution is strongly influenced by cultural perspectives—as gender expressions and styles have varied greatly across cultures and throughout history. Some children experience strong feelings of hurt or shame when they experience gender attribution that does not match their gender identity. Others are not bothered. Unless we are conscious about our own assumptions and we create a culture where children are given agency to identify their own genders, we are likely to make incorrect attributions to some of the children in our programs.

Gender attribution in action: what does it look like?

Sara was legally designated female at birth. However, growing up, the gender attributed to Sara was frequently male (i.e., Sara was often assumed to be a boy). Sara was even pushed out of a girls' restroom in elementary school by another girl who thought she was a boy. When adults and children heard the name "Sara," they were often confused as Sara is not a typical Western name for a boy in a US cultural context. Being seen as male was confusing, painful, and a source of shame for her growing up. In fact, more than one substitute teacher accused her of misbehaving or acting up when she raised her hand after hearing her name called for attendance. Their attribution of a male gender to Sara was so strong that even her own testimony ("Yes, my name is Sara") was not enough to change her teachers' minds that she must have been trying to play a joke on them. Now, as an adult, Sara identifies as both male and female, but the female piece of her identity was hard fought despite it being her legal designation.

Young children might talk about gender attribution by saying:

- "Sometimes people look at me and think I am _____ [a girl, a boy, don't know]."

- "Sometimes people call me _____."

Teachers might help young children reflect on gender attribution by saying:

- "When people say that, how do you feel?"

- "Why did you guess that person is a girl?"

Misgender

To misgender someone is to refer to them as a gender that is other than their gender identity. This often happens when an individual assumes a person's gender (gender attribution) based on their impression of them. Misgendering often comes in the form of using the wrong pronouns for a person. When misgendering happens as a mistake, it is fine to simply apologize and correct oneself without making it into a big deal. Intentional or malicious misgendering can be very hurtful and invalidating for a child.

Young children might talk about the experience of being misgendered by saying:

- "Everyone thinks I'm a girl because I have long hair, but I'm a boy. Boys can have long hair too!"

- "I'm a girl, but my teacher always calls me a boy and tells me that boys can't wear dresses."

- "I don't like it when people call me 'he.'"

Sexual orientation

This term is included here only because it is so often confused with gender. Sexual orientation and gender are not the same thing. Gender is personal (how one sees oneself, "Who I am"), while sexual orientation is interpersonal (who I am attracted to physically, emotionally, and/or romantically). One of the most common ways the confusion between gender and sexual orientation shows up is when young children who are assigned male show interest in behaviors considered to be feminine (gender expression). Jen, a 24-year-old nonbinary person assigned male at birth, recalls: "I used to carry a doll as a child. I don't know much about the doll—just that my parents thought dolls would make me gay."[9]

Gender and sexual orientation are, however, related to one another. Societal beliefs about what is acceptable or normal in terms of gender have implications for sexual orientation as well. For example, many adults communicate strong messages to young children about what it means to be a boy or girl (gender identity), how boys and girls should behave (gender expression), and who they should be attracted to as they grow up (sexual orientation). Thus, from children's youngest years, they receive messages from adults about the relationship between gender and sexual orientation. It is essential for early childhood teachers to understand that gender and sexual orientation are two separate aspects of identity:

- Transgender or gender expansive individuals can have a range of sexual orientations including gay, bisexual, queer, straight, or others.

- Similarly, individuals with different sexual orientations (gay, lesbian, bisexual, etc.) have a range of gender identities (e.g., cisgender, transgender, nonbinary, and more).

Gender and sexual orientation: distinct but interrelated aspects of identity

While gender and sexual orientation are separate identity categories, they are very much interrelated. Members of minority groups from both categories have struggled alongside each other for recognition and rights in many countries. The umbrella acronym of LGBTQI+ (lesbian, gay, bisexual, transgender, queer, and other marginalized identities) is used occasionally in this book to refer to all individuals who are not both cisgender and heterosexual—the dominant identities. It is important to remember that, while gender and sexual orientation are often grouped together in this way, they are entirely different aspects of one's being!

While sexual orientation is not the focus of this book, we believe it is important to achnowledge that homophobia—fear of, and power exercised against, non-heterosexual orientations—is pervasive in early childhood education settings.

> *Some people think sexuality has no place in the early childhood classroom and therefore we shouldn't talk about it. But we do all the time—every story where a princess marries a prince, every set of toys that contain a man and a woman and a baby: these are giving messages about sexual orientation. The message is that heterosexuality is normal. We need to counter this message by showing what a range of sexuality looks like, in age-appropriate ways. So, we're not talking about what people do in bed; we're talking about all the kinds of attraction and romantic relationships that happen, including queer relationships and also people who have multiple romantic relationships at the same time, or none at all! –Kira, Kindergarten Teacher*

Heteronormativity

This is the cultural assumption that all people fall into opposing gender categories (male and female), and that they will be attracted to people of the opposite gender.

Intersectionality

Gender is an essential aspect of children's identities, and can only be understood in relation to other aspects of identity. Children are developing as whole beings and their understandings and experiences with gender are interrelated with other aspects of their identity (i.e., social categories including their race, ethnicity, socioeconomic class, sexual orientation, citizenship, religion, age, primary language, ability/disability, and other factors). Acknowledging these distinct but interconnected aspects of identity is the foundation of intersectionality (Crenshaw, 1989; 1991). Intersectionality recognizes that an individual's position, or membership in different social categories, impacts their identity formation and experience of privilege and/or marginalization. For example, the identity development of a young Black gender expansive child would be significantly different than a white gender expansive child because the Black child would face discrimination related to race and gender—experiences that would increasingly influence a child's developing sense of themselves and their accumulated trauma.

Intersectionality is not only about privilege and marginalization. It also recognizes other ways our experiences differ based on our unique positions in the world. For example, that same Black child might have different references for masculinity and femininity based on their family's values and norms than the white child might have. And a Black child raised by queer, disabled college professors in a rural setting would have different gender references than a Black child raised by straight restaurant workers in an urban Baptist community. And so on. **It is our job as early childhood teachers to support children's sense of validation and pride in all their identities, including those of their families** (Derman-Sparks & Olsen Edwards, 2010). A child is more than any one of their parts.

Young children might reflect their intersectional identities by saying:

- "I'm brown, just like my mamas! My family comes from _____."

- "In my family, all the boys grow really long beards and wear turbans."

- "I want to wear pretty dresses like Angelica, but my mom says we can't afford them."

Gender: putting it all together

I identify as...	Gender identity. "What I feel like inside. What I know my authentic gender to be." Boy, girl, transgender, agender, boy-girl, in-betweener, sometimes boy/sometimes girl, neither boy nor girl...
Please call me...	Pronouns: She/hers, he/his, they, theirs...etc.
My body has...	Anatomy and physiology: Penis, vulva, etc.
When I was born, people thought I was...	Legal designation at birth Female, male, third designation (in some locales)
Now people look at me and see...	Gender attribution
And I want them to see...	Gender identity and gender expression
My favorite toys, games, clothing, hairstyles are...	Gender expression
My other identities and experiences are...	Intersectionality: Religion, race, socioeconomic status, ability/disability status, etc.

As you are learning, gender is a lot more than a pair of check boxes! Below we introduce several metaphors and models for representing the slowly evolving changes in societal attitudes, beliefs, and understandings about gender and all its component parts. These metaphors do not comprehensively represent every cultural belief system related to gender. Instead, our goal is to illustrate a significant shift seen in Western cultures in the last two decades. We also realize that different readers will be coming in at different points along this progression of gender models, and we find that it's helpful for folks to see each of the steps along this path rather than jumping over some of them. We acknowledge that the concept of gender is dynamic and will evolve over time as children and adults continue to reveal to us new layers of understanding about what it means to live in a just society that values gender diversity. By the time you are reading this book, we're sure we will have tweaked our model again to account for our own new learnings!

Gender boxes

 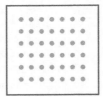

- Boy
- Referred to as "he"
- Has penis and testicles
- Has more testosterone
- Is attracted to girls
- Doesn't cry
- Plays with trucks
- Likes roughhousing

- Girl
- Referred to as "she"
- Has vulva
- Has more estrogen & progesterone
- Is attracted to boys
- Feelings! Tears!
- Plays with dolls
- Wears dresses

Binary boxes: A visual tool to illustrate the gender binary. It features a pink square containing rows of pink dots and a blue box containing rows of blue dots. Credit line: Julia Hennock.

In this model, all the component parts of gender that we defined (anatomy, physiology, identity, expression, legal designation, pronouns, and sexual orientation, which we know isn't even part of gender!) are bound up together and predetermined by external genitalia at birth. You are placed in a single gender box with strict walls around a set of ideals and expectations governing all the elements of gender. These ideals and expectations prescribe what a child's anatomy and physiology should look like and the preferences they should have in activities, clothing, career paths, sexual desires, and more as they grow up. If an individual performs their assigned gender correctly based on these ideals (including physical development), gender attribution is expected to come easily for others who meet them. In this way, it is often seen as your fault if someone else cannot immediately tell which box you belong in because you have failed to meet the expectations laid out for you at birth.

As you now have a broader sense of the different aspects of ourselves that combine to make up gender, you can see how a **gender binary** where there are only two choices does not accurately represent the range of variation that actually exists. Many cultures across the world and throughout history have acknowledged three or even more genders (see box near start of Chapter 1). However, Western cultural beliefs have largely only acknowledged two, and the gender binary is still the primary belief system about gender around the world.

The ideals and expectations in the gender box model are all but impossible for any individual to adhere to in reality. We have a hard time believing anybody has reached adulthood without trying to stick an arm or a leg outside of their prescribed box at some point, although society has a lot of ways of reprimanding you when you do that! The gender binary, with its solid and unbending boxes, is damaging for everyone. Can you think of a time when your gender was regulated by others because you were not being "manly" or "womanly" enough according to someone else? How did it feel to be pushed back inside the box when someone else thought you had reached out too far? Have you ever seen someone who you couldn't immediately put in a discrete binary gender box? How did that make you feel? The impossible ideal of two gender boxes is damaging to all of us, and extremely dangerous for those who don't fit (or can't squeeze themselves) neatly into one of them.

It is worth noting that there are many people who are not opposed to the idea of transgender folks climbing out of the box they were given at birth, as long as they climb all the way out of that box and get all the way into the other binary box. Even many transgender people hold a binary view of gender. However, when we think of all the possible combinations of identities, expressions, bodies, and more, it becomes clear that trying to force everyone into only two boxes is simply not adequate.

Gender as a spectrum

Male	Nonbinary/Agender	Female

The concept of gender as a spectrum rejects the boxes view as too simplistic and failing to capture the wider variation of genders that exists among children and adults. A gender spectrum positions male/masculine on one end and female/feminine on the other; this model allows for people to position themselves anywhere along the spectrum. Someone can identify in the middle (equal amounts feminine/female and masculine/male *or* gender neutral/agender), lean towards one side of the spectrum (more feminine/female than masculine/male or vice versa), or locate themselves on one extreme or the other (only feminine/female or masculine/male). The spectrum allows for an acknowledgment of fluidity as well, since individuals can change where they position themselves on the spectrum over time (Gender Spectrum, "The Language of Gender," 2017). This was the first Western model to introduce individual agency to define oneself, but it still uses the gender binary as a framework, and all the individual components of gender that we have defined are still bound together. This limits how gender can be understood.

Gender as multiple spectrums–the Genderbread Person

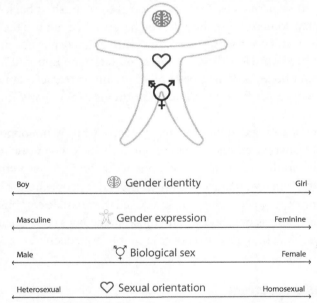

Gender as a Genderbread Person: A visual tool that features a gingerbread-person-shaped figure. This figure's gender identity is connected to their brain, their biology to the genitals, and their gender expression to the body. Gender identity, biology, gender expression, and sexuality are accompanied by binary-based spectrums to show the complex, independent nature of these facets of gender and sexuality.
Credit line: itspronouncedmetrosexual.com.

While the original spectrum model included only a single scale for gender, the TGE community and researchers of gender diversity began to break gender down into all the component parts we have discussed. Models such as the Genderbread Person became popular to show the various elements of identity, expression, and anatomy and physiology (shown in this model as biological sex) as distinct yet interconnected pieces of the greater picture of gender. Sexual orientation is shown in these models as a separate spectrum, independent of gender identity or expression. In this model, we begin to see more possibility in combining various identities, expressions, and bodies as they are no longer tied to one another like they are in the boxes or on the single spectrum model. An individual may have a body that was labeled male at birth, identify as female, and enjoy wearing cargo shorts and baseball jerseys that are typically coded as masculine. This model continues to build on agency and diversity in our understanding of gender.

Many TGE community members and educators acknowledge the limitations of the gender spectrum model, and have sought to improve or replace it with other models. One commonly observed limitation is that the spectrum model continues to rely on two oppositional concepts (feminine/female vs. masculine/male—the gender binary!) to make sense of gender. The implication is that a move towards "boy" is a move away from "girl," and this does not fit everyone's experience. Another limit to the model is that it views gender in a vacuum, isolated from the other facets of a person's identity and position in the world.

Gender as spinning a web

Gender as a web: A visual tool which recognizes that gender is a deeply personal and individualized concept for children and adults, and that no two webs are identical. Adapted from Ehrensaft (2016b).

Diane Ehrensaft (2016b) introduced a new model for understanding gender in her book *The Gender Creative Child*: a web that is woven actively by each individual child with three major threads—nature, nurture, culture—and a fourth factor, time. The theory of gender as a web recognizes that gender is a deeply personal and individualized concept for children and adults, as no two webs are identical. Gender is understood to be individually constructed, and in this way, Ehrensaft's model distinguishes itself by giving children agency beyond a binary in creating their own unique webs.

According to Ehrensaft (2016b), "Nature includes chromosomes, hormones, hormone receptors, gonads, primary sex characteristics, secondary sex characteristics, brain, and mind" (p. 25). This maps closely, though not exactly, with what we refer to as anatomy and physiology. Nurture includes "socialization practices and intimate relationships, and is usually housed in the family, the school, peer relations, and religious and community institutions" (p. 25). This includes all the ways children are treated and taught to behave as a result of their legal designation at birth and the community in which they live. And culture includes "a particular society's values, ethics, laws, theories, and practices" (p. 25).

What it means to be female or male, feminine or masculine, varies from culture to culture across the globe and throughout history. The final element of Ehrensaft's model is time—acknowledging that "we all, you and I and everyone around us, will always be tweaking our gender webs until the day we die" (p. 25).

Compared to the spectrum models, the web model is better able to capture the dynamic way an individual actively shapes their gender (identity, expression, and more) over the course of their life. Gender webs offer an infinite number of combinations of these threads, and so diverges from the gender binary even as it is represented in the spectrum models. Another element of the web model that is unique is that a web can be damaged. According to Ehrensaft, if others "grab the thread of the web from us as we are spinning it, and tell us what our gender has to be, rather than listening to us as we spell out our gender, or rather than watching us do our own creative work, we are at risk of ending up with a tangled knot of threads, rather than a beautifully spun web that shimmers and glows" (p.25). This aspect of the web model allows us to talk about a child's **gender health**—something that is missing from previous models of gender.

What is gender health?

Gender health is the opportunity for a child to live in the gender that feels most real and/or comfortable for them. Gender health includes the ability for children to express their gender without being rejected, criticized, ostracized, or restricted from living their authentic gender selves.

(Hidalgo *et al.*, 2013; Keo-Meier & Ehrensaft, 2018)

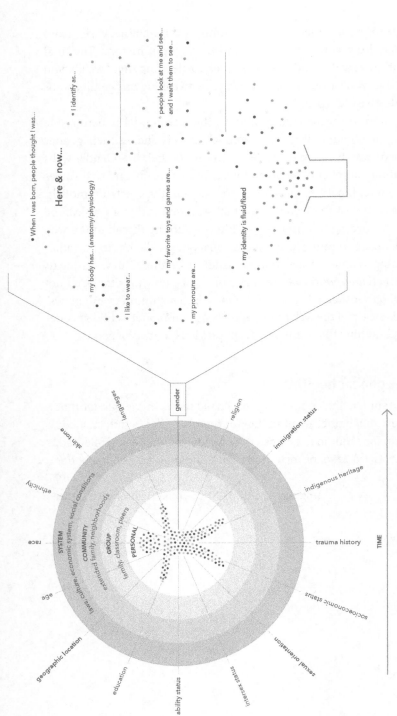

Gender as an intersectional constellation: This is our evolving gender model. It is not based in the binary; rather it prompts us to describe our gender by completing phrases related to our current gender identity, anatomy, gender expression, and more. In this way, we understand our gender as unique, its parts connected (and often changing) like a constellation. It looks at gender as it relates to our various identities and sociopolitical contexts. Credit line: Julia Hennock.

The blank lines are for filling in with your gender attribute

---

When I was born, people thought I was...

· I identify as...

Here & now...

people look at me and see...
and I want them to see...

my body has... (anatomy/physiology)

my favorite toys and games are...

I like to wear...

· I like to wear.

· my pronouns are...

my identity is fluid/fixed

languages

gender

skin tone

religion

ethnicity

immigration status

SYSTEM
laws, culture, economic system, social conditions

indigenous heritage

race

COMMUNITY
extended family, neighborhoods

GROUP
family, classroom, peers

PERSONAL

age

trauma history

TIME

socioeconomic status

geographic location

sexual orientation

education

intersex status

ability status

Intersectional gender constellation

The Gender Justice model of gender combines elements of both the Genderbread Person and Ehrensaft's web. It also expands upon these models to reflect our intersecting identities and the systems of power and oppression that affect us as a result.

Like the Genderbread Person, we recognize that there are many component parts of gender—identity, expression, anatomy, physiology, legal designation, pronouns and language, and attributions. However, we do not see any of these factors as existing on simple linear spectrums. These factors are represented in our model in open-ended reflections for each individual child to fill in using all the many ways that very young children communicate (not just by verbally finishing the prompts). There are also unwritten bullet points to show the facets of gender yet to be discovered and invented by children. Each of those bullet points are represented by dots, once tightly bound by the walls of an assigned gender box, now shown floating freely in our image of the child. You might imagine these facets of a child's gender moving like particles, shining like stars, clustering in the air and forming dynamic constellations that shift and rearrange over time. This view of gender breaks free of the binary entirely and offers the greatest possible agency to children as they form their own unique gender constellations. These gender particles mix and mingle with particles representing all the component parts of a child's religion, ethnicity, trauma history, race, and every other intersecting identity they hold—each of which is just as multifaceted and individual as gender.

Like Ehrensaft's web model, we recognize socialization and culture as influences on gender. We also emphasize the dynamic nature of gender shown in Ehrensaft's model by the image of a child actively weaving the threads of nature, nurture, and culture together. In our model, this active agency over time is captured by open-ended gender components and the movement of the entire image through a child's lifetime, starting from a particular point in history. At any slice along that timeline, a person's gender might look different.

However, gender must also be understood as intersectional in relationship to other aspects of an individual's whole identity. Culture is not monolithic or consistent child to child, even between two children growing up in the same neighborhood. It is important to understand how gender expression, identity, and other components might vary by race, class, sexual orientation, age, ability/disability, immigrant/migrant status, and more. These multiple identities and characteristics are shown as spokes intersecting through the child.[10] As the child moves through their life, different spokes might be closer to the foreground of their experiences while others move to the back for a while. For those who live in poverty, the stress of simply meeting basic survival needs can overshadow other intersecting identities in many ways. Perhaps a child who has needs related to their gender health can't differentiate that particular pain from their hunger or lack of sleep related to poverty.

A person might hold relative power or experience relative oppression on any of these spokes, based on the values of their communities during their lifetime. For example, in most Western cultures at the start of the 21st century, some privileged identities and characteristics include whiteness, maleness and masculinity, Christianity or having no religion, being able-bodied, heterosexuality, cisgender identity, financial wealth, being a non-immigrant, and more. For most of us, it is easier to recognize the areas where we experience relative oppression or marginalization, because the unfairness is highlighted in our own eyes. However, learning to see where we each hold relative power and privilege is a critical step in helping to fight for justice for everyone. Intersectional oppression is not simple math, though. We can't just count up our privileged identities, subtract our marginalized ones, and see where we stand. But it is extremely important to understand that gender-based bias and oppression cannot be considered in isolation from other systems of power and oppression.

A child's unique profile of intersecting identities and characteristics, power, and marginalization makes up the middle circle of our model—the **personal** influences. We further break "culture" down into increasingly wider circles of influence on the child. As teachers, our first point of contact with children is in the next circle: **groups** the child belongs to. This includes all the social circles with which a child has regular and direct contact—family, classrooms, playgroups, religious groups, and other close relationships. In this circle, our own intersectional identities and areas of power or marginalization inform how we make assumptions about and gender attributions for children.

Moving further out, children are influenced by their **communities**: extended families, neighborhoods, local politics, geographical location (urban or rural environments), etc. Beyond this layer, children are influenced by the **systems** in which we all live—laws, economic structures, social hierarchies, language structures, and more. The gender binary exists in this layer in Western society, as it is embedded in so many of our systems. Someone whose first language is Spanish will grow up internalizing a gender binary that extends beyond people to inanimate objects, as most Spanish nouns—along with the nouns of all Romance languages are designated as either masculine or feminine regardless of context. When we look at gender within an intersectional framework, we can more deeply understand how power structures are built into our systems and perpetuated through each circle of influence on children.

Supporting children's gender health in an intersectional model

Now that we have completely reframed gender from the old boxes model, what is a teacher's role in supporting children's gender health?

Colt Keo-Meier and Diane Ehrensaft sum up a few of the key points to remember in their Gender Affirmative Model (GAM) (2018). Central to the GAM is the evidence-based idea that **attempting to force someone to live as a gender with which they do not identify does that person harm.** Instead, the GAM supports children's gender health by creating the opportunity for children to live in the genders that feel most real and/or comfortable for them and by giving them the freedom to express gender without experiencing restriction, criticism, or ostracism.

A gender affirmative approach supports all children's gender health. The GAM is based on several beliefs (Keo-Meier & Ehrensaft, 2018):

- No gender identity or gender expression is pathological (wrong, "sick," needing to be "fixed").

- Gender identities and gender expressions are diverse and vary across individuals and cultures. Supporting children's gender health requires cultural sensitivity and culturally responsive practice.

- Gender is a complex integration of biology, development, socialization, culture, and context.

- Gender can be fluid or fixed. When gender is fluid, it can change for an individual over the course of their life. Additionally, these changes can take place at different times for different people.

The classroom culture can be a place where children get to explore gender in a way that they don't in certain other areas of their life. It's such an opportunity to create a culture that can create a new norm in the world. —Encian, Preschool Teacher

Our job as early childhood teachers is NOT to categorize or try to determine children's gender identities. This will feel uncomfortable for many adults as it is ingrained in us to try to categorize and label others. Teachers can and should acknowledge this difficulty. However, it is our responsibility to create early childhood environments where children are supported in exploring their genders without pressure from adults to categorize themselves. Equipped with your new expansive understanding of gender and what you are learning about gender health, it is your job to advocate for children's right to build their genders in loving, supportive environments with adults who see and celebrate them for who they are.

How will teachers learn what children are thinking and feeling about gender?

Children have many ways of communicating with us about how they are making sense of the world around them—what they find interesting, puzzling, concerning, frightening; what questions they have; and the forms of support they desire. If teachers take time to observe and listen to children, they will discover that children are sharing their thoughts and feelings about gender in their **verbal and nonverbal interactions** (their language, stories, gestures), **in their play** (the pretend play themes, who they include/exclude in their play, the play materials they use), and **through their participation in the expressive arts** (painting, drawing, movement/dance, music/singing, writing, theater/acting/pretending). Throughout the chapters of this book, teachers will learn how to tune in to what children are communicating to others about gender and how they can respond to children with messages that are gender affirmative and support all children's gender health.

Why have I never heard about gender diversity or how to support TGE children in any of my classes and textbooks?

It is true that most early childhood teachers are only exposed to child development research and descriptions of best practices that ascribe to the binary gender boxes model. The majority of early childhood teachers learned about children's gender development using theories and empirical research that have now been significantly challenged as inaccurate and, in many cases, harmful. Therefore, an important step in the process of creating gender justice is "unlearning" information about children's gender development based in outdated theories and beliefs.

Unlearning traditional theories of gender development

The process of creating gender justice in early childhood must include a conscious unlearning of traditional child development theories and the beliefs and assumptions about gender we now know are not accurate. The first step in this unlearning process is to examine how traditional theories of gender development in early childhood have shaped early childhood teachers' beliefs about what is typical/atypical, appropriate/inappropriate, and normal/abnormal for young children. As you will see below, some of the taken-for-granted assumptions in these traditional theories are not only inaccurate; they can also be harmful if and when they are used to **misgender** children and/or create environments that do not support all children's gender health.

Some of the gender myths represented in child development and early childhood textbooks, and reflected in the assumptions of many adults that need to be unlearned, include the following.

Myth: **Anatomy and physiology determines one's gender.** Traditional gender theories reinforce the idea that anatomy and physiology determine a child's gender. Further, these traditional beliefs associate pathology (mental illness) with anyone who rejects the gender that was legally assigned to them at birth. This leads to the stigmatizing and shaming of any child who does not identify as cisgender and express their gender according to the strict norms associated with the gender binary.

Myth: **Gender identity is determined in early childhood and is stable throughout an individual's lifespan.** Lawrence Kohlberg's (1966) theory of gender constancy claims that young children realize their gender identity—that they are either male or female, and dictated strictly by genitalia—by the age of three. The next stage he claimed happens at about four years of age when children begin to understand that gender is "fixed" or stable, and they will still be male/female when they are older. Finally, between the ages of five to seven, Kohlberg asserted that children begin to understand that changes to clothing, names, or behavior will not change a person's gender. Kohlberg believed that children first learn that gender is permanent or constant, and then they use this understanding to learn to behave in "gender-appropriate" ways. Kohlberg's theory of gender constancy has been widely cited in child development courses as the most important developmental theory related to children's gender development. As a result of Kohlberg's theory of gender constancy, children whose gender identities and gender expressions fall outside of traditional male/female categories have been perceived as atypical in their developmental progression, pathologized, and assumed to be destined for lifelong negative consequences.

Kohlberg's theory of gender constancy has been widely disputed and is not supported by the evidence emerging from contemporary research studies on young children's gender development. Current research highlights that gender diversity is the norm and that gender is much more complicated and individualized than traditional Western developmental theories like Kohlberg's work represented. While identity does develop in early childhood, it is not tied strictly to anatomy, and it is harmful to children to force them to accept gender roles and identities with which they do not align.

Myth: Children 0–5 years old are too young to know their gender identity. Oddly, many people subconsciously hold both beliefs that children must know and accept their genders in early childhood (as proposed by Kohlberg), and beliefs that early childhood is too soon for children to know their gender identities. The catch is that they usually consciously hold whichever one works against TGE children in a given context. When working with young children, many people will subtly or not so subtly enforce Kohlberg's theory—directing children into their designated boxes and making sure those children "know" exactly what their gender is (by assignment). Then, when faced with a transgender child who is very confident about what their gender is, the same people will claim that this child is too young to know. This invalidation of TGE children comes so naturally that most people don't even notice the contradiction.

In Black families we have these sayings about being soft or about "having sugar in your bowl…" and so from a young age, I had some sugar in my bowl, and I was soft. At age four, I had a doll and I would take the doll to church, and it was my grandpa's church and it was like, "People are gonna think you're this way if you carry a doll with you," and I was like, "I don't care. I'm gonna carry my doll." –Jen, Nonbinary person thinking back to early childhood

Myth: Young children are too young to understand or learn about oppression. Traditional child development theories—for example, Piaget's (1958) stage theory of children's cognitive development—created images of children as naïve and egocentric, unable to see a situation from another person's point of view. These theories influenced decades of thinking about young children as too young and intellectually immature to have much awareness of their own participation in social categories (gender, race, etc.). As a result, it was also assumed that young children were incapable of participating in intentionally harmful or oppressive interactions (racism, classism, sexism, etc.). We now know from research that children at very young ages have an awareness of various social categories of identity and that they understand and read the cultural norms that associate some social categories as privileged (e.g., being white, English speaking), and others as marginalized (being a person of color, immigrant, etc.) (Terry, 2012). Studies have shown that children reproduce oppressive dynamics in their play and other interactions with each other (Zosuls *et al.*, 2009). It is our belief that, if children are capable of reproducing these oppressive dynamics, then they are old enough to learn about them in order to disrupt them. As always, teaching young children should be done at an age appropriate level, focusing on concrete experiences and what is fair and unfair.

The process of unlearning these myths and shifting one's understanding of gender will take courage and persistence. It is worth the effort! Throughout this book we will share strategies that you can use to notice and disrupt the assumptions and myths about gender that are harmful. We will talk about what you can do to communicate to every child in your care that it is safe for them to be authentic whenever they are in your presence.

REFLECTION TIME

Young children are already thinking about gender.

– What ideas do you have about what children know or don't know about gender?

– What assumptions have you heard from friends and relatives when they talk about children's ability to understand their own gender?

– What could you say to address these assumptions in the future?

Adults do not determine children's identities.

– Next time you're with young children, observe the way that others address them. What do you notice about the messages adults are sharing with children about gender? What messages do you hear that reinforce the gender binary and cisgender experience as normal and anything else as pathologized?

– Think about your own language. Does the language you use support children to authentically express their gender identities?

– What is a step you could take to help reduce the circumstances (language use, messages in the environment, lack of representation, etc.) that may be creating stress and trauma, and lead to the development of gender-related shame for children?

Why Early Childhood Is Such an Important Time to Talk about Gender Diversity

Because gender identity develops between ages one-and-a-half and three years (Ehrensaft, 2016b), access to information about how to work with transgender and gender expansive children is essential for professionals who work with young children (Gonzalez & McNulty, 2010).

The early childhood years, and especially the first three years of a child's life, are uniquely important because this is the most sensitive period for children's brain development. The experiences a child has during this time shapes the architecture of their brains. Through healthy and caring relationships where adults help children feel safety, a sense of belonging, and the freedom to explore their environment, children are supported to build the brain connections they need for learning and healthy development. Similarly, early experiences with prolonged stress and trauma can lead to impaired brain development for young children, with negative outcomes that can last a lifetime unless there is effective intervention.

We know from research and reports from TGE adults that many young children also know that their authentic genders are not aligned with the genders originally assigned to them. **TGE adults report that they knew they had to hide their authentic gender self from their families, teachers, peers, and communities as young as the age of two** (Steele, 2016). Living with this type of secret, where children have to hide their authentic gender identity on a daily basis from the adults who are caring for them, is exactly the type of situation that can create so much stress and trauma for young children that their brain development is negatively impacted.

Research suggests[11] that early childhood is a critical time for children's gender development. Here is why...

By 12 months:

- Children begin to categorize individuals by gender (Quinn *et al.*, 2002).

There is no biological or intellectual reason why children categorize gender as boys/girls. They do this because they are reading the social norms of the world around them. If they grow up in environments that are inclusive of gender diversity, they will learn from the earliest ages that gender is not restricted to a binary.

By 18 months:

- Children begin to understand their gender identity (Halim, Bryant, & Zucker, 2016).

Given children's emerging awareness of their gender identities, it is critical that adults observe, listen, and not claim to know children's genders based on their gender expression or their anatomy.

By 2 years:

- Children can communicate awareness that their gender identities are incompatible with their legal designations (Steensma, Biemond, de Boer, & Cohen-Kettenis, 2011; Steensma, McGuire, Kreukels, Beekman, & Cohen-Kettenis, 2013).

- Children begin to recognize gender stereotyping, which may be displayed through toy preference or an expectation for other children to present gender a particular way. For example, children may invalidate or reject a boy wearing a dress (Zosuls *et al.*, 2009).

- Children consistently attribute genders to others based on the gender-boxes model during categorizing picture activities (Zosuls *et al.*, 2009).

By 2½ years:

- Most children have awareness of their gender identity and can communicate about it using language ("I am a boy", "I am a girl", "I am an in-betweener," "I am a boy and a girl," etc.). Children understand how they are feeling inside about their gender (I am happy to be a girl) (Halim, Bryant, & Zucker, 2016).

By 4 years:

- Children construct a personal belief system of gender stereotypes that is reinforced by cultural and social norms (Halim & Ruble, 2010). For example, children may have strong feelings about what male or female tasks are, such as cleaning or fixing something. This may be seen in their play or descriptions of experiences (Halim, Bryant, & Zucker, 2016).

As you can see, young children are not only old enough to start talking about gender; they will also have already formed foundational understandings of themselves and the world of gender by the time they leave your program. If you don't start talking to them about gender in an affirmative and justice-based way, they are bound to soak up the restrictive and oppressive norms of the gender binary system we live in.

We all have agency to influence change. Working for gender justice requires courage and it is continuous and long-term work. And it is essential that all early childhood teachers begin their own personal journey to learn about gender diversity so they can support all of the children in their care to thrive. Each chapter in this book will provide you with information and strategies for becoming a champion for gender justice. We hope you enjoy your learning journey!

--- Chapter 2 ---

Attuned and Responsive Relationships

We return to our friend Lucien, who has spent many days now borrowing clothes from the extra clothes bin labeled "girls" and who plays every day with Emma, pretending to be sisters. Emma and some of the other children have started using "she" and "her" to refer to Lucien even outside of dramatic play, which Teacher Heather has noticed and jotted down. She wants to make sure to bring it up with her co-teacher, Meg, at their check-in on Monday so they can figure out the best way to support Lucien.

However, that Friday, while Teacher Meg is helping children settle into lunchtime, she overhears a conversation happening at one of the tables. Emma is talking to the group at her table about the contents of everyone's lunchbox. When she gets to Lucien's, Emma says, "Lucien also has grapes, but she has more than me. And hers are green, but mine are purple." Teacher Meg asks Emma to repeat what she said. Emma looks startled, and shrugs. "Did you call Lucien 'she'?" Emma looks at Lucien and back at Teacher Meg. She nods. "Why are you saying 'she'? Does Lucien want you to call him 'she'?" Both children say nothing and appear to be uncomfortable with the question. Other children have quieted and are listening to Teacher Meg.

"Lucien, do you want to be a girl? Should I let people know that you are a girl?" Lucien looks down, shrugs, and mutters, "I don't know. Yeah?"

Teacher Meg raises her eyebrows in surprise. She was not aware of the sister play, and had not heard the children using she/her pronouns for Lucien before. Wanting to support Lucien, she turns to the class, and announces, "Everyone, Lucien wants to be a girl. Does everyone understand that for now, Lucien is a girl?" The children nod their heads.

Lucien is very quiet for the remainder of lunch, and later builds in the magnet tiles area with Emma. They do not play sisters that day.

Both Heather and Meg care for Lucien and want to be supportive, but Meg missed the opportunity to really attune to Lucien's emotional state and needs. What Meg did in this example is called "outing someone" (see box), and outing a transgender child without their consent and agency over when and how and to whom they come out can be extremely dangerous—both internally for the child and in the potential for social backlash and bullying or violence. By not attuning to Lucien, Meg created a very painful experience for her, even though Meg had good intentions.

Outing

"Outing" someone is based on the phrase "coming out" (or "coming out of the closet"), which is when someone tells others about their gender identity or sexual orientation. Since these two identity categories are not inherited or necessarily also held by any family members, and since our society assumes every child to be cisgender and heterosexual until proven otherwise, the act of coming out is typically required if a child who is not one or both of those things wants others to know their true identities. While we hope the work you do towards gender justice will eliminate some of the stigma and pressure that makes coming out such a stressful time for individuals, we know the world is not yet at a place where revealing one's transgender identity is a simple and carefree decision process. Whether a child comes out, and to whom, is a very personal and individual decision. Outing a transgender or gender expansive child without their consent and explicit control (over when, how, and to whom) is a dangerous and effectively violent act, even when done with the best of intentions. We will discuss strategies for when and how to talk to children about whether they would like to come out, but we want to emphasize the child's agency as being central to this process.

Caring responsive adult–child relationships and attunement, are foundations of gender inclusive classrooms striving to create gender justice for all children. It is the central responsibility of all early learning professionals to develop attuned relationships with all children and their families in their care. You might be wondering: What is attunement? And how does it relate to building strong relationships with children so they feel a sense of belonging and safety as well as feeling supported to live as their authentic gender selves? Let's explore answers to each of these questions below.

What do we mean by attunement?

The most important foundation of a high-quality inclusive early childhood program is for children to be able to interact with a caring, responsive, and self-regulated adult who attunes to them. Attunement is defined as the process of an adult focusing so intently on what a child is communicating that the child comes to believe that what they think and feel matters: they "feel felt" by the adult (Levine & Kline, 2007). The adult's genuine interest in the child acknowledges and validates the child's presence and helps the child to feel a sense of visibility, safety, and belonging. If an adult is curious about the child's thoughts, perceptions, and authentic feelings, then the child will come to value and trust their thoughts and feelings as well.

Tuning in to a child to understand what they are thinking, feeling, and communicating is central to attunement. When we "tune in" or attune to a child, we show genuine interest in understanding what the child's emotional state and/or behavior is communicating (Stern, 1985). Attunement begins when we focus in on a child's emotional state, carefully observe a child's verbal and nonverbal expressions, bodily movements, and gestures (or lack thereof), and ask ourselves questions about what they see: "What story is this child communicating to me about how they feel and/or about what they need in order to feel a sense of safety, belonging, and/or agency?" When we are attuned to children we respond to children's communication with interest, curiosity, and a sincere desire to understand what they are communicating. Attuned adults are able to express empathy for children's perspectives and desires and make choices that strengthen the child's feeling of trust in our presence.

The experience of attunement begins in infancy through what is described as a **serve-and-return relationship** between a child and their adult caregiver(s) (see: https://developingchild.harvard.edu/science/key-concepts/serve-and-return/). Attunement can be thought of as a dance. Infants are continually communicating to adult caregivers how they feel and what they need—the "serve" (e.g., crying, cooing, showing interest by looking at something, turning their head away when overstimulated). Attuned adults "return" the serve by responding to young children using words or gestures (e.g., eye contact, tone of voice, picking them up, facial expressions, focusing their attention, handing them objects). By repeating serve-and-return cycles continually and daily, young children learn critical lessons about whether adults listen to and care for them. Children learn whether they can trust their caregivers to be available and attuned—

providing support, encouragement, and a sense of belonging and safety in moments of need and as they interact with their environment.

"Adult Meets Child Where They Are": Beginning at birth, when adult caregivers take the time to attune to a child's needs, strengths, and experience with the world around them, a safe environment is created in which to explore, learn, and express their authentic selves. Credit line: Jonathan Julian.

Attuned interactions are the foundation for building self-esteem and a strong sense of self for the child. When serve-and-return patterns are positive and support children's healthy development, young children learn that they are loved and cared for, will be protected by their caregivers, and that they are important members of their family and community. These messages support children to develop a positive sense of themselves, which is essential for their ability to form trusting and healthy relationships with others. When we do not listen carefully to what children are communicating about what they want and need, or when we respond in ways that create a sense of fear and stress for children, we create an environment that lacks safety and the ingredients for trust to form. This might look like a child showing distress and an adult responding with an angry tone of voice, a harsh touch, or by ignoring the child and their attempt to communicate about what they need to feel safe and loved. Children in these environments learn very early that their needs will not be met by their caregivers, and that what they think, believe, and want do not matter. This not only harms their emerging sense of themselves, but also leaves a vulnerable child feeling that they have no control over their environment, that they are unable to trust adults to take care of them, and that the world they are living in is an unsafe, unpredictable, and threatening place. This sense of hopelessness can disrupt a child's healthy brain development and negatively impact their ability to form healthy relationships with others.

Perhaps most of your interactions with children follow the basic pattern of attunement, but you are not able to acknowledge and "return" a child's "serves" in certain areas that trouble you or where you have little experience and awareness—such as exploring gender identity and expression. The "serve" may be subtle, or unrecognizable, if you are coming from a gender binary mindset. The child may still grow to trust you, but chances are this trust will come at the expense of hiding a part of themselves from you. See the section "What happens when adults don't listen to children" later in this chapter for a discussion of what happens when we do not listen to what children are telling us about themselves and their genders.

Emotionally attuned interactions with young children begin with observation and following a child's lead

Ashline has just turned one. She is crawling towards the Tonka truck in her family childcare setting. Talia, her caregiver, comes over with a cat puppet and engages Ashline's attention. "Meow, meow, I'm hungry! Can you feed me please?" She animates the puppet, and Ashline stops playing with the truck to pay attention to the puppet dancing around in front of her.

In this instance, Talia is probably not consciously aware that she has redirected Ashline, a (presumed) girl in her care, away from what she was expressing interest in—gross motor play with a truck—towards an object and activity that the caregiver has selected: dramatic play with a puppet. Perhaps Talia's unconscious associations between boys and trucks, and girls and dolls[12] have made it difficult for her to see what is actually happening. Regardless of the reason, Talia is not attuned to Ashline.

To attune to a child, early childhood teachers will carefully observe what the child is communicating. Teachers will respond in ways that reinforce to the child that their presence, needs, and desires are acknowledged and important to the adults caring for them. An attuned interaction with Ashline would start with observing what she is communicating about her interests and then following her lead. What would this look like for Talia? Talia could carefully observe

Ashline and notice that she is interested in playing with the trucks. Talia could then communicate to Ashline that she is "in tune" with her interests by commenting on what she sees Ashline doing: "Oh, Ashline, you see the big blue truck! You're pulling yourself up on the truck. Oh, it moved! That was surprising!"

By commenting on Ashline's play, Talia sends a message to Ashline that acknowledges her presence in the group and reinforces that her choices and actions are valued by the adults caring for her. By tuning in to focus on Ashline's interests and initiative, Talia teaches Ashline that she can trust her caregivers to be responsive to her needs and desires. These messages create a healthy foundation for Ashline's developing sense of self.

When we attune to children, we support them to be narrators of their own experiences. In addition to following a child's lead, attunement involves what Bronwyn Davies (2014) calls emergent listening. In most of the conversations throughout our day, we "listen in order to fit what we hear into what we already know" (p. 21). We do not expect, and often therefore we do not allow, our underlying worldviews and central beliefs about "the way things are" to be shattered and rearranged in our day-to-day interactions. Davies calls this "listening as usual." Emergent listening, on the other hand, "means opening up the ongoing possibility of coming to see life, and one's relation to it, in new and surprising ways" (p. 21). To Davies, true listening—emergent listening—is about "being open to being affected" by what one hears, rather than simply responding. The concept of emergent listening is deeply inspired by and built on work by Carla Rinaldi (2012), president of the Reggio Emilia Foundation, on the importance of listening for mutual learning to occur.

This type of listening requires us to trust children as capable of narrating their own experiences. Through gestures, play, artwork, verbalizations, and children's "hundred languages" (Edwards, Gandini, & Forman, 2011), children communicate their perspectives, concerns, desires, solutions, and understandings of who they are and what they experience in the world around them. This requires us to maintain open hearts and open minds. Trusting children will undoubtedly challenge many assumptions that we have about who we assume or imagine children are. Attuning to young children asks adults to start by listening mindfully to children and remaining open to what they tell us, especially if their stories challenge our beliefs and taken-for-granted assumptions. When we remain open to changing our minds after tuning in to a child, and open to whatever we learn as a result, we communicate a powerful message to children that they will be acknowledged and supported by their caregivers as they explore and make discoveries about who they are and how they belong in their families and communities.

Davies validates that "Emergent listening is demanding. It means not confining oneself to opinion, or to what one has always believed or wanted. It involves the suspension of judgment, letting go of the status quo" (2014, p. 28), which in our case may mean letting go of a firm grip on the gender binary to hold a child's hand as they lead us into the gender unknown.

What does it look like to express love over respect for a child?

Dan is the father of Zed, a four-year-old child—presumed boy—who loves wearing dresses and jewelry in the costume corner at school, and has begun to ask for similar clothing at home. Dan expresses his concern about this behavior during a parent–teacher conference. "I love my son," Dan states simply. "This dress up might be okay here, but I don't want him to get teased next year when he goes to kindergarten. I know how children are," he adds. Dan asks teachers to discourage Zed's dress wearing. When teachers question the fairness of denying materials to one child, he suggests they remove all the dresses from the costume corner. The teachers agree. In the following weeks, Zed, along with other children in the class, continue to fashion dresses out of large scarves.

While most parents, like Dan, care deeply about their children, this instinct does not always lead them to provide the type of supportive environment a child needs. If a child's authentic gender is not understood or accepted in a parent's or teacher's worldview, the adult may act in ways they believe are protecting the child, but are actually causing greater harm as they steer their child down a path of shame and hiding. **Caring about children is not enough.**

David Hawkins, MD, PhD, explains the difference between love and respect: "The more magic gift is not love, but respect for others as ends in themselves, as actual and potential artisans of their own learnings and doings, of their own lives... Respect resembles love...but love without respect can blind and bind. Love is private and unbidden, whereas respect is implicit in all moral relations with others" (Hawkins, 2011, p. 79). In other words, while our love for someone may compel us to speak or act for them, we cannot do right by them until we respect them as their own unique person with the agency to speak and act on their own. In the instance above, we can see how Dan's love for Zed, combined with his fear of possible future violence, prevents him from fully seeing Zed in his present joy, and leads him to advocate for circumstances that stifle Zed's exploration and growth. To truly support his son, Dan must reframe the way he is seeing Zed, from a potential victim to an "artisan of [his] own learning and doing"—that is, a child forging their own path.

Early childhood teachers should communicate messages of both love AND respect to children

Love: The feeling of deep affection for someone or something, and the way we show them that feeling.

Respect: Honoring and acknowledging another person's actions, opinions, or ways of being in the world as valid, whether or not we agree with or understand them.

Applying this to gender means...
When a child communicates gender identities or expressions that are beyond our comfort level or understanding, we still honor what they are doing or saying, and trust that they are the expert on themself.

According to Hawkins, respecting children requires us to offer them our resources (including our time and skills, such as when we travel with a child to a TGE playgroup), contribute to their "learnings and doings," and seek out and value their accomplishments, no matter how small they may appear (2011). Respect in this light is fundamentally about extending or helping children grow and expand—rather than constricting or putting limits on what a child is able to do. To help visualize this distinction, imagine that the child is a stream formed by snow melting on a mountain top. The stream is heading towards a cliff. An adult who loves the stream may decide to protect it by building a dam, so that it forms a pond and never reaches the cliff. But an adult who respects the stream might feed their own water into it so that it is able to flow over the cliff with such fullness and force that it forms again at the bottom, finding shape once more.

What might a love-*with*-respect response have looked like?

If Dan is worried about future bullying, he would do better to provide Zed with a safe space in which to be himself, wear what he wants, and feel supported in his gender expression, so that if bullying occurs in the future:

- Zed will be more confident and better equipped to respond to it.

- Zed will trust Dan to provide critical support and to act as an ally, who understands and respects his son and advocates for his son's needs.

- With this trust, Zed will be more likely to open up to Dan about bullying that happens.

If Zed knows that his home is a safe place to wear dresses, he and Dan can have open conversations about bias that exists outside those walls. Dan can affirm and assure Zed that this bias is unfair and that the problem is not with Zed but with how other people think sometimes. Together they can come up with a plan that allows Zed the freedom to explore his gender expression and also the agency to decide whether or not he will sometimes wear other clothes to help keep him from experiencing that bias. This practice of navigating the world not only in one's authentic gender in spaces that are safe, but also in a more stereotypically gendered way around people who harbor strong gender biases, is similar to the concept of code switching (Auer, 1998). (See box below.)

Dan can partner with Zed's teachers to help make school another safe zone. With this approach, as opposed to the original story, Zed learns that he is loved, respected, and valued for his gender expression. He is also meaningfully involved in the decisions that affect his own life. And, since conversations are held openly with Zed, he will be much less likely to make assumptions that lead to shame than if the subject is avoided or discussed behind his back—implying that his gender expression itself is the problem rather than social bias.

Code switching

Code switching (Auer, 1998) refers to the practice of altering between two or more languages or speech patterns depending on who you are talking to or the setting you're in. It is a practice discussed at length in studies of race in America, where communities of color speak one dialect of English with each other but have learned to "talk white" around white people due to racism and racial bias.

Children have demonstrated the capacity to understand that different spoken and unspoken codes of conduct as well as speech patterns exist among different people, places, and situations. Children may face violent and hostile reactions to their gender expressions in their neighborhoods, homes/living quarters, schools, and other environments. As teachers, we should not pressure children or their families to have them embody their full gendered selves in places where they do not feel safe. Instead, we can ask children and families questions about how they feel in these different spaces and help them brainstorm strategies for getting their needs met. While it is critically important that children have at least one safe place where they feel supported to be themselves, there is still much work to be done to transform all spaces to support children's gender health. This is why it's so important that we create these spaces in our programs, and work with families to create them elsewhere!

I feel like that's a more helpful way of navigating gender with children who are experiencing really aggressively intense binary spaces. How can we at least give them check-ins and let them know that we are watching out for them, so that when situations happen they know they can bring it back to us to process it? And we can create a model of what allyship looks like, so that they know that there are other outlets rather than just rage or conformity in response to bias. -Mitali, Teacher

Parents are not the only ones who must remember to balance their love for children with an equal measure of respect. Let's look at another example.

Martin is a shy and quiet three-year-old who rarely takes social risks. But today, he is the first (presumed) boy in his class to try on a dress from the dress-up rack at his school. The dress he picks is pink and sparkly. One of his teachers, Mary-Anne, approaches him. "Oh, Martin!" She exclaims. "Aren't you just adorable in that dress! Let me take your picture."

In this case, Mary-Anne is reacting in a positive way to Martin's gender exploration, and she would certainly characterize her response as loving. However, there are a few problems with her approach. For one thing, **she is objectifying Martin—treating Martin as an object to be admired for his look, rather than a person with agency.**

Objectification

This happens when you treat a person as if they were an object, instead of engaging with them as a thinking, feeling, "learning, doing" human being. When we treat a young child as if they are a doll for us to dress up and fuss over, we are sending them a message that their value is not in the way they think and do but in the way they look. Objectification is most commonly linked to gender bias through the widespread objectification of women and girls. Have you ever noticed yourself complimenting girls on what they are wearing or how they look ("I love your sparkly dress!"), while complimenting boys on their capacities to act ("You're so strong!")? Many studies have shown that this type of differential feedback for young children based on gender is common from adults.

Additionally, since Martin is shy and quiet and rarely takes social risks in the classroom, being the first presumed boy in the class to take a dress down off the rack was probably a pretty big decision for him. By drawing attention to Martin's choice of wearing a dress in this way, Mary-Anne demonstrates that she was not attuned to him. She runs the risk of embarrassing Martin and causing him to shut down or stop his explorative behavior and to withdraw into himself. The writers of this book have seen firsthand how children can shut down after ostensibly positive reactions to children taking gender risks—from one child who stopped wearing dresses, saying "I don't like when people call me 'cute'," to Lucien's experience from the beginning of this chapter. Even if Martin doesn't react in a negative way to Mary-Anne's public comments, other children who hear them might quietly choose not to explore gender expression in class because they don't want similar attention.

Even more subtly, by drawing attention to the fact that Martin is wearing a dress, **Mary-Anne is making a statement to both Martin and the class that this is exceptional behavior—out of the ordinary.** Without intending to, Mary-Anne is undermining a gender-diversity message by framing a boy wearing a dress as an exceptional occurrence rather than as part of play-as-usual. While this may not seem like a big problem, this sort of small instance reinforces a stronger social message that dictates that "Gender conformity is normal, gender transgression is not," and leads children to view themselves as one of the "regular" people, or someone "different."

The counter-message, which is essential for children to hear and see again and again, is that everyone is different, and our differences are what make us unique. Simultaneously, everyone shares things in common (Derman-Sparks & Olsen Edwards, 2010). A possible statement that supports a diversity rather than exceptionality approach, which Mary-Anne might use in response to questions from other children or parents is: "Many children like to wear dress-up clothes. Today Martin is trying on a dress, and Leon is trying on a construction vest."

But what would an attuned, love-with-respect response that supports children's gender health look like, in this situation?

First, Mary-Anne need not comment on Martin's choice of dress up at all. The attuned teacher often waits for the child to make the first gesture in the dance of attunement, or cycle of serve and return. This is not the same as ignoring Martin. Avoiding a response to Martin or reacting negatively (frowning at him) would be an example of a **microaggression**, communicating a message of disapproval or discomfort with his choice—a reaction that could negatively influence his developing sense of himself and compromise his feelings of safety and belonging. Being attuned to and respecting Martin's shy demeanor, Mary-Anne could communicate her pleasure in Martin's exploration without drawing undue attention to it by making a small, positive gesture (e.g., a smile, or thumbs-up). Or Mary-Anne could make a descriptive comment to extend Martin's play, as she would for any child, "Oh, Martin. Look how the light bounces off the shiny places on your dress. It's making a pattern on the wall!" This sort of comment lets Martin know that Mary-Anne sees and accepts his action, without treating it as out-of-the-ordinary or objectifying him and overlooking his agency.

What is a microaggression or microinvalidation?

Microaggressions are the everyday slights and insults that people in marginalized groups endure and that most members of the dominant group don't notice or take seriously. They can be "intentional or unintentional and include verbal, nonverbal or behavioral, or environmental indignities that communicate hostile, derogatory, or negative connotations about a particular culture or group of people. A gender microaggression is a subtle negative attitude conveying that one's gender identity is less valuable than the dominant culture's defining identities" (Lubsen, 2012). First coined by Chester M. Pierce, MD in the 1970s, the term microaggression has grown significantly in its use, as has our understanding of the effects that microaggressions can have on their targets. Microaggressions are usually unconscious, and harm can be unintentional. Even if we have the best of intentions and are actively learning, we will still make mistakes and be responsible for microaggressions. Sometimes a microaggression is an insult that is buried in the underlying assumptions of a statement. When a child tells a boy he "throws like a girl," there is the direct and intentional insult to that boy, but there is also the microaggression towards all girls and feminine children that doing something "like a girl" is somehow shameful.

A microinvalidation is a comment or action that excludes, nullifies, or negates a person's experiences, thoughts, or feelings based on his or her membership in a marginalized group. Their impact is to make people feel invisible. They are particularly harmful forms of microaggressions because their targets are shamed and made to think that they are paranoid or oversensitive when they react negatively to the microinvalidation. An example would be an invalidation of a person's attempts to communicate their experiences. If a young child, presumed male, tells you "I'm a girl!" and your first response is, without stopping to tune in to the child, "That's great, Sean, but it's not time for playacting right now," there is a chance that you have invalidated Sean's experience by not taking the communication seriously or even plausibly. Since each instance is, by definition, very small, targets are usually told to simply brush off the harm. However, this request is itself a microaggression—asking an individual not to have an emotional response to being hurt. Also, the cumulative effect of experiencing countless tiny wounds over time can be deep and lasting—impacting self-esteem, physical health, mental health, and more (Sue, 2010).

What are examples of microaggressions and microinvalidations related to gender?

- Misgendering someone by using pronouns or other gendered language (like sir, ma'am, dude, lady, etc.) that are not in line with how a person wants to be addressed.

- Making a subtle scowling face at a boy putting on a princess dress or stopping a child from engaging in an activity or experience due to gender: "Nail polish isn't for boys."

- Dressing a child only in skirts and dresses, then discouraging active play.

- Listening in order to categorize or respond instead of listening with a willingness to be affected when a child is communicating about their gender.

- Preventing individuals from using a gender-identified bathroom. "This is the girls' bathroom. Please go to the boys' bathroom next door."

- Insisting on categorizing people as "boys" or "girls": "Are you a boy or a girl?", "Good morning, boys and girls!"

- Making statements that assume a binary and dependent relationship between gender and anatomy and physiology, and which invalidate or negate transgender existence (e.g., "Today we're going to look at the female anatomy" and having this only include vaginas and ovaries, when many females have different anatomy).

- Drawing attention to a TGE person's anatomy and physiology without their consent.

- Using a person's old name if they have transitioned to one that better suits their gender (this is often called a "dead name" in trans communities).

> • Squinting your eyes at someone or looking uncomfortably long at their body as you try to figure out their gender.

In order to make a comment about the way the light is hitting Martin's dress, Mary-Anne would have to slow down enough to notice it in the first place. She would also have to observe what Martin is doing, so that she could decide whether such a comment would help him extend the exploration of his body or distract him from something else he is engaged with. **Either way, the foundation for a teacher's response that communicates respect is paying attention to the child.** In other words, the adult who wishes to respect a child as David Hawkins describes—by valuing, supporting, and extending their doings and imaginings—must first take time to notice them. This noticing, or paying attention, is an important piece of **emergent listening** and **attunement**. Let's look at another example:

Hal, three, is playing by himself in a sandbox. Luke, a teacher, sits nearby. "I'm a kitten," Hal suddenly announces. Luke responds, "Hello kitty." Hal pauses, then continues: "I'm a flying kitten." The teacher replies, "Ah, a flying kitten." After another pause, Hal adds, "I'm a flying kitten named Felix." The teacher smiles. Hal is often a flying kitten named Felix. "I'm a flying kitten named Felix who's a girl. A girl kitten." Hal looks up at his teacher, a grin spreading wide across his face. Luke smiles back and comments, "I see. You're a girl kitten named Felix. How do you fly?" Hal lifts his elbows: "See my wings?"—and flies off.

Notice that in this instance, Luke did not draw special attention to Hal's gender choice—a first for this child, presumed male, who until then had played male characters. Luke also refrained from making any value judgments about Hal's ideas (i.e., he did not judge or evaluate them), beyond the encouraging gesture of the smile. This doesn't mean Luke had no thoughts about a child he perceived as male playing a girl kitten; if he did, he kept them to himself.

Notice also the pacing of this serve-and-return interaction, as it was filled with pauses. By paying attention, repeating back Hal's ideas, and giving Hal time and space to expand them, Luke was demonstrating a deep attunement with Hal. **Luke created a space in which Hal felt valued and knew that what he was saying was being truly heard.** Luke was engaged in emergent listening. He probably doesn't really think Hal is a cat with wings, but he allowed Hal's creativity to emerge and he was listening not just to respond but to see where Hal took him and to honor that space.

We can imagine how the interchange above may have progressed differently had Luke rushed Hal, "Okay kitten, I have to go put sunscreen on Adelaide and Lamora," or brushed him off, "That's nice." Carla Rinaldi notes that "the most important gift that we can give to the children in the school and in the family is time, because time makes it possible to listen and be listened to by others" (Edwards, Gandini, & Forman, 2011, p. 235). Of course, it is challenging for a teacher to create this sense of time and spaciousness when they have conflicts, injuries, and the multiple needs of a class of children to attend to. Emergent listening and deep attunement in the moment are always ideals to strive towards and a set of practices to be continually aware of and committed to strengthening. Let's explore what this type of listening could look like between co-workers in an early childhood program committed to gender justice.

Susan is a teacher in her mid-50s. She has seen a range of gender expressions among children over the years, but has never had the language to describe it. She is uncomfortable with the idea of a child's gender identity changing from their legal gender as designated at birth. A child in her class, Lolo, has recently asked to be called "she," at home and at school. Lolo's single mom supports her child's request. At a staff meeting, Susan describes the difficulty she's having with this transition. "It just feels wrong to call him 'she' when he's always fiddling with his penis!" There is a younger, transgender teacher on Susan's staff named Tara. Tara explains how this child's gender identity has nothing to do with her body, and how painful it feels to any individual when their gender is not accepted by others. Susan listens.

For Susan to hear her co-worker's words and allow them to affect her pronoun use with Lolo is no easy task. Associating genitalia with gender is something that most of us, cisgender or otherwise, do immediately and unconsciously. Even those of us who were raised to be unconstrained by gender roles have typically been taught something along the lines of: Having a vagina/vulva makes you a girl, and having a penis makes you a boy. This message is comforting to most cisgender individuals because it feels clear-cut in most cases. It is part of our illusion of certainty that holds up a mostly uncertain world. However, for many TGE individuals, it is a profoundly uncomfortable insistence, because it does not match our experience of the world. If Susan engages in a typical, surface kind of listening, she may hear this sentiment as her co-worker expresses it, and acknowledge it, saying "I hear you are saying that it is hard for you when someone calls you by the wrong pronoun." Yet engaging in **emergent listening requires the listener to be open to being changed or affected by what they hear or experience, possibly in a fundamental way that challenges their convictions and worldview.** It is this deeper listening that we strive for in our interactions with co-workers, family members, and children, and which we strive to cultivate between and among children in our classrooms.

If Susan is engaged in this deeper form of listening, she might hear the connection Tara has to Lolo's experience, having likely lived it herself. She might imagine a world in which she herself felt at odds with the gender everyone around her perceived her to be, and how painful that world would feel for her. If Susan listens, not just to respond or to categorize, but to be changed by what she hears, she might start to shed her need for a binary and stable understanding of gender to make space in her heart for Lolo—just as she is.

As we practice **emergent listening**, we must be sensitive to ways that others express themselves beyond direct verbal communication. Young children (as well as adults) also communicate through gesture, vocalization, movement, eye contact—and through what Loris Malaguzzi, a main founder of the Reggio Emilia educational practice, describes as the "hundred symbolic languages" of children: drawing, sculpting, shadow play, dramatic reenactment, storytelling, finger painting, and building in the sand and mud, among many others (Edwards, Gandini, & Forman, 2011). What adults tend to consider an artistic medium, the child reveals to be, at its core, a mode of expression and communication. As teachers and caregivers, we must tune into these "hundred languages" as closely as we listen to direct verbal conversation. Let's look at another example.

Zayla's preschool class has been dictating stories and acting them out during group time. The girls in Zayla's class have primarily told stories about princesses and fairies, and the boys have focused on stories about ninjas and superheroes. Zayla—a presumed girl—has written a series of stories about a knight who searches for a dragon that hides in various places (a cave, a tree, a chimney). She casts herself as the knight, who uses "he/him" pronouns. As she enacts these stories with her friends, they begin to choose her for "boy" parts in their own stories—princes, brothers, guards, and others. Zayla takes on these roles with gusto. Soon, she takes on these roles outside of story-acting time, during free play, as well.

In this case, Zayla has been listened to by her classmates. Although she has not said, "I am a boy" or anything along those lines, her story writing and acting has changed the way her peers perceive and relate to her gender. Her positive response encourages them to keep moving in that direction without explicit request from Zayla.

What happens when adults don't listen to children?

When children take in messages from all around them about gender and how boys and girls are supposed to be, feel, look, and act, and when those messages do not align with how they feel themselves to be deep inside, they start to internalize those messages as shame. According to shame and vulnerability researcher Brené Brown (2007), "shame is the intensely painful feeling or experience of believing that we are flawed and therefore unworthy of love or belonging" (p. 69). TGE children start to learn very quickly that they are not like other children who were assigned the same gender box that they were, and those differences can be viewed either as something to celebrate, or as an aspect of who they are that they feel they need to hide. We hope that one outcome of this book will be that more TGE children will be taught to celebrate their genders before they internalize all the "shoulds" and "supposed tos" as shame.

Shame (Brown, 2010; 2017)

1. We all have it.

2. Nobody wants to talk about it.

3. The less you talk about it the more you have it.

Clinicians and researchers agree that shame is the root of much suffering in society including such conditions as addiction, trauma, aggression, depression, eating disorders, and bullying. The good news is: We can decrease our internalized feelings of shame when we talk about them with others. Our shame cannot survive when we are attuned to and given empathy from others. Even if the young children we work with have already started developing shame about their genders, we can combat that force with open conversation about it. We can let them know that they are valued for who they are, including their genders.

While the word "trauma" often evokes images of big negative events in one's life, research shows that smaller everyday traumas trigger the same neurological response. Brown believes that "many of our early shame experiences, especially with parents and caregivers, were stored in our brains as traumas" (p. 89). Shame triggers a child's stress response system just like trauma, sending them into an automatic and involuntary fight-or-flight survival mode. Donald Nathanson (1994) further mapped shame responses in his model—the compass of shame. This research-based model describes the four main categories of behavioral responses people exhibit when they experience shame, which tie closely to the fight-or-flight model (see following Figure). These categories include avoidance, withdrawal, attacking others, and attacking the Self:

- **Avoidance** (flight): This range of responses does not simply mean avoiding others, but can mean avoiding connection, closeness, or authenticity out of fear of being rejected or shamed again. These children may even become eager for attention but rarely show their deepest selves to anyone.

- **Withdrawal** (flight): Withdrawal responses, similar to avoidance, are based in fear of what might happen if other people see too deeply inside us. These children may be seen as shy and quiet. They might fly under the radar of the adults around them, and indeed this is likely their goal.

- **Attacking Others** (fight): Shame can just as easily turn to anger as it can to fear. Children may act out and be aggressive towards the person or people who they believe caused them to feel as badly as they do. Shame is such an intensely painful and uncomfortable feeling, it is hard not to be upset with whoever you believe is responsible for your feeling that way.

- **Attacking the Self** (fight): If one internalizes that same responsibility, it can lead to self-hatred and self-disgust. If a child takes on external messaging that they are flawed in a way that is disgusting, disordered, or deficient, it is a very quick road to self-harm. As we saw with the grim statistics shared at the beginning of this book, far too many of our beautiful TGE children walk down this path. (Nathanson, 1994)

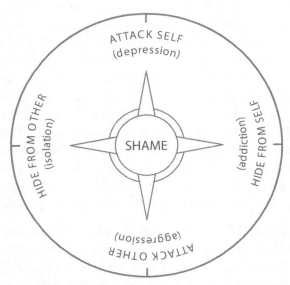

Compass of shame: A visual tool to help understand some of the impacts of shame, which closely mirror the impacts of traumatic stress. In this image, we see that the impulse to fight, flee, or freeze is a common experience and reaction to shame, just as it is to trauma. Adapted from Nathanson (1992) and Taylor (2015).

We believe it is likely that any TGE child who has experienced gender-based shame, regardless of which point of the compass of shame they tend towards, is unlikely to continue expressing their gender openly after a point. That point may be very early in their gender development and exploration. While many teachers wait until a child announces that they are transgender to begin making changes in the way they address gender in their programs (Payne & Smith, 2014), this strategy will leave behind all the young children who are already hiding their genders because they have internalized shame. To connect back to attunement, the "first serve" in a child's gender exploration and communication may be extremely subtle. If our return generates shame because we didn't see it for what it was, we might not get another chance.

We cannot have attuned relationships with young children if we are not aware that they may be trying desperately to hide a central aspect of themselves from us out of fear and shame. As early childhood teachers, we need to create environments that prevent children from developing shame about who they are. Our professional responsibility to every child is to support them to feel respected, visible, safe, and protected in our care. By creating environments that normalize gender diversity and support children to explore their genders openly, we can help to prevent gender-based shame and trauma for children in our care.

Growing up, there was a story my father would tell occasionally about how my dislike of feminine things started very early in my life. I was only two or three years old when my dad dressed me for the day in what he thought was a nice, cute denim skirt. I made it a few steps out of my room and down the hall before I realized I wasn't wearing shorts. I threw a tantrum in the hall and utterly baffled my poor dad, who had no idea what he had done wrong. Being required to wear stereotypically "girly" clothes in my childhood was always a difficult and traumatic event. I remember crying about those clothes right up until the end of high school when I discovered the other half of the department store. I hid in a bathroom stall for over an hour during a sports awards ceremony my freshman year in high school because I had worn a dress and couldn't face my friends. The feeling of wanting to crawl all the way out of my skin when I had to wear girls' clothes started very early for me and never faded. It was a terrible, visceral feeling, and I can only assume that's what I felt that day in the hallway with my dad.

In this example from a transgender adult, we see a child's serve of rejecting feminine clothes met with distress and confusion by a loving father. In this case, the "serve" may have been loud, but the father had no awareness of gender diversity to draw from in his attempts at attunement. Later in adolescence, we see shame responses of withdrawal, and the disgust related to attacking the self in response to situations in which feminine clothes were required.

How shame develops in early childhood: research with transgender and gender expansive adults thinking back to their earliest memories related to gender.

Steele (2016) completed a participant action research (PAR) study examining how four adults who identify as transgender or gender expansive described the messages they received in their early childhood years about gender identity and gender expression. In a PAR study, attention is given to who is studying and who is being studied, as well as what will be done with the findings. In many PAR studies, those being studied—traditionally the subjects—become actively involved in dissecting the meaning and value of the data collected. For Steele's study, the four participants (including Steele) worked together to identify themes that came up, and discussed ways these findings could be used to make positive change for TGE individuals, including being used in this book.

Multiple sources of data were collected for the study including individual journal entries, focus group discussions, and individual participants' interviews with their family members about their earliest experiences related to gender. Results of the study illuminate how shame can develop among very young children when they perceive it is not safe to reveal their authentic gender self. **Feelings of shame and a perception that they needed to hide their gender identities and gender expressions from others were experiences that all four participants recalled having throughout their childhood.** And these feelings started from a very young age, for some as early as their toddler years.

Shame and hiding were the two most prominent themes in the conversations, journals, and communications with family members in Steele's study. The study participants remembered feeling a deep and urgent need to hide their internal experiences and desires to exist as a different gender than the one assigned to them, especially after experiencing being shamed for breaking gender norms. They also recalled having their attempts at communicating their authentic gender selves overlooked or dismissed out of hand as impossible or simply the result of their childhood imaginations. Sophia, a trans woman in her 60s, describes her experiences related to shame and hiding, which began in her early childhood years.

Sophia recalled playing dress up with her older sister at their grandfather's house as a young child. Her sister was adorning her with makeup, a wig, a stuffed bra, shoes, and a skirt. Sophia loved it until her sister wanted to show her off to their grandfather. Sophia remembers the look on her grandfather's face seeing her dressed as a girl. She explained, "I knew immediately that it was a mistake. I flew back up the stairs and out of those clothes, hot with shame." Without a word, Sophia's grandfather had conveyed the degree to which she had broken the social rules for a young boy, and the shame Sophia felt was swift and strong. What had been a playful exploration of gender expression for Sophia and her sister, and what had felt both fun and affirming to Sophia, quickly became something she knew she could never do again.

Sophia only remembers a few stories of this nature, where she expressed herself or presented herself as somehow other than male as a child. The message from those few experiences was strong enough that she learned to ignore and repress those feelings and desires. Sophia did not come out as transgender until she was 58, married, and with grown children. She remembers her marriage counselor suggesting that she might be transgender and her wife encouraged her to think about it. To Sophia, it was the first time in her life she had been granted permission to explore who she really was. She explained, "It felt like I had been building a dam my whole life, and once I got permission to take out a brick and see what was behind it, it just flooded over me." Until that moment, she had worked diligently to hide, dismiss, repress, and deny who she was under the fear of being seen again as she had been seen that day by her grandfather.

The message Sophia received from her grandfather's wordless reaction to her outfit is received by gender expansive children in countless interactions every day of their lives. The "rules" of gender may not be written down (though sometimes they are!), but when they are broken, it stirs something deeply ingrained in most people. These responses are not always ill-intentioned or even conscious, but they can be felt deeply by a child who experiences them.

One study of elementary school teachers and administrators found that "fear and anxiety are common educator responses to the presence of a transgender child and the disruption of the gender binary" (Payne & Smith, 2014, p. 399). In a lecture from the Black Minds Matter series discussing the experiences of Black boys in education, Dr. Luke Wood (2018) describes the type of subconscious body language a teacher might exhibit in the presence of a Black male student that conveys fear and anxiety based on stereotypes and the "smog" of bias. He claims that "you cannot teach, you cannot counsel, you cannot advise someone that you fear because it will mar all the micro-level interactions that you have with them." We believe this is similar to—while also distinct from—the type of fear, anxiety, discomfort, and even disgust experienced and expressed (verbally or nonverbally) by teachers working with TGE children as well. These (typically subconscious) feelings can be sensed by a child, and they not only limit the ability of that teacher to create a safe learning environment for that child, but also can be internalized by the child themselves. **When this happens, children can learn to believe that there is something wrong with them that scares or repulses others.**

Themes from Steele's (2016) PAR research study

Shame and hiding. Feelings of shame and hiding their gender expressions and gender identities started in their earliest years. These two feelings were embedded in, and woven throughout, all the experiences the transgender and gender expansive adults recalled from their early childhoods.

Bullying and ostracism. All participants described external experiences of bullying, ostracism, and many negative experiences with peers, starting as early as preschool.

Gender identities, behaviors, and expressions imposed by others. Being consistently told by others about who they are, who they couldn't be, and what they could or could not do was experienced by all participants. Impositions constraining and defining their gender identities, accepted behaviors, and gender expressions were commonly experienced. These are forms of aggression and invalidation that began at birth, or even earlier.

All of these themes suggest the critical importance that early childhood environments be focused on gender justice from the earliest days and that teachers should not wait until they recognize a gender expansive child in their classrooms to create inclusive programs and cultures—especially given the shame and hiding many transgender adults report having experienced as young children.

Yet most early childhood programs have no training for teachers on TGE children. The ones that do have trainings usually develop those trainings in response to a child already in their care being brave enough to come out as transgender or in response to the arrival of a transgender child into their program (Payne & Smith, 2014). Because teachers are waiting for children to come out as transgender in their classrooms and childcare programs, most support is **reactive** rather than **proactive**. As a result, many gender expansive children (as young as two years of age), are busy developing strategies to hide who they are inside. When they do attempt to communicate about themselves, they are more often than not being ignored or dismissed or not truly heard in an emergent listening or attuned sense of the word. We are allowing gender expansive children to hide in fear and shame when we do not provide them with the language, safe spaces, and trust required to tell us who they are and the openness to truly listen when they do. By being reactive, we are also putting the responsibility of creating the language and the space for that type of communication onto young children who may fear for their safety—physically, emotionally, psychologically—should they ask for what they need or tell us who they are.

Creating a space where all children learn about gender diversity, explore gender in open and creative ways, and discuss gender stereotypes and bias with a critical lens is good for every child. We have all had our gender constrained in many ways throughout our lives, starting in early childhood and carrying on through adulthood. Cisgender women are critiqued for being too outspoken or too demure, too fat or too thin, for how they dress, and for choices they make about their bodies, their own children, their careers, and more. Cisgender men are ridiculed for expressing tenderness and vulnerability, for being unathletic, for being soft or girly. There are many forces that promote conformity to gender norms that impact all young children. A learning space that is both attuned to children and nurturing to gender expansiveness provides:

- safety for all children to explore who they are

- life-saving affirmation for children who are transgender and gender expansive

- a greater capacity for empathy and understanding others in children who are cisgender and fall more easily into society's accepted gender norms.

This attuned and nurturing environment requires teachers to reflect deeply on fear and anxiety they may hold about having a transgender child in their program or about having open conversations about gender expansiveness with children, parents, co-teachers, and their administration. Teachers must not only offer love to the children in their care. They must also respect those children as narrators of their own lives, and listen with an openness to being changed by what children communicate about their genders and their experiences. By raising our own awareness about the shame and hiding that TGE children experience, we can learn to see and interrupt microaggressions and invalidations before they cause shame. We can work actively to create spaces where children feel safe and supported in their gender explorations.

Self-study and classroom audit tool: relationships and interactions with children, families, and peers

Use the statements below as a guide to think about the ways you interact with children (statements 1–7), families and caregivers (statements 8–20), and other teachers and staff in your program (statements 21–25). If your response to any of these statements is "Of course I do!" we encourage you to think critically about ways you could continue to improve on that area. Nobody is perfect, and we all operate from a position of assumption and bias based on our own experiences, no matter how long we do this work! Consider how children, families, and peers might answer these statements about you as well. There is always room for growth, and recognizing this is one of the best things we can do for children!

1. I treat children with care and respect. I pay attention to what children do and say, and value their contributions to the classroom.

2. I allow children to explore genders beyond the gender binary. I don't insist on all children being a boy or a girl.

3. I affirm children's gender expressions and identities, without drawing undue attention to choices, expressions, and identities that cross social norms.

4. I approach children as equal partners in co-creating a culture of gender creativeness and exploration.

5. I believe that children are the experts on their own gender and experiences, and I respond to children accordingly. I trust children every day; even if what they said yesterday was different, what they're saying today is not wrong.

6. I allow children to set the pace on if/when they want to share their gender identity with others. I never "out" a child without their explicit consent and dialogue with the family.

7. I notice how I am treating children differently based on gender, and I make sure I actively contradict stereotypes.

8. I treat parents and family members with respect. I pay attention to what family members do and say, and value their contributions to the classroom.

9. I take the time to ask/learn from families about their family structures, traditions, and norms. I stay respectful and stay curious.

10. I am willing to adjust my curriculum each year in response to the needs of families.

11. I provide resources about the language I plan to use around gender at the beginning of the year, solicit feedback, and begin conversations with families who have questions, concerns, and input.

12. I approach relationships with families as partnerships in supporting the gender health and growth of their children together.

13. I resist holding the role of "expert" in how children should do or experience gender.

14. I communicate a holistic awareness of each child, remembering that gender identity is just one aspect of a child, not their whole being. When I talk with families I tell them many things about their child. I do not focus exclusively on gender.

15. I introduce families to gender diversity resources.

16. I share ongoing information about read-alouds, conversations, and conflicts that emerge in the classroom around gender, including the language I use to respond.

17. When conflicts arise, I listen to family members' opinions and feelings without judgment. I validate these feelings and attempt to uncover underlying motivations.

18. I talk about the strengths that come from children's gender expressions and identities rather than "problems" associated with them.

19. I advocate for children's gender health and well-being.

20. I utilize the support I have (school mission, NAEYC (National Association for the Education of Young Children) professional code of ethics) in enacting my professional responsibility to address gender justice with colleagues and families.

21. I instigate and encourage discussion about children's gender exploration with my co-workers.

22. I work to create a classroom culture in which teachers communicate with and understand one another about approach to gender.

23. I foster continuity and consistency in the way teachers respond to children's gender exploration.

24. I use methods of observation and documentation to reflect on children's gender exploration, taking notice of language they use to describe themselves and each other. I share and discuss my observations with my co-workers.

25. I solicit feedback and support from students, parents, and colleagues on how my gender bias shows up in the classroom, recognizing that this is an ongoing process.

—— Chapter 3 ——

Strengthening Self-Awareness to Check Assumptions and Interrupt Biases about Gender

Diversity [is] a way of life rather than a problem to be solved or fixed by casting the other as deficient. (Dray & Wisneski, 2011, p. 28)

People are often looking to learn and be trained around what children need. What children need are adults who have done our own work around our gender and our racial identities. We cannot expect students to tell their stories and bring their full selves if we're not doing that. (Kate, Early Childhood Equity Trainer)

"Doing our personal work is essential, and the children will lead us, step by step if we are open to observing and paying attention to what they are telling us. There is a lifetime of learning for every one of us teachers - but if we stop looking at our own experiences, our own beliefs, our own hopes and fears - we close down our ability to truly support and cherish the children we serve. (Julie Olsen Edwards, co-author of Anti-bias Education for Young Children and Ourselves, 2010)

Becoming an early childhood teacher committed to creating gender justice for young children and their families begins by **strengthening your self-awareness and having the courage to discover and explore your own authentic gender self as well as your personal assumptions and biases.** This work is urgent and critically important, and by reading this book, you are taking an important first step to becoming a more connected and attuned teacher for all of the children in your care. This work requires a high level of emotional engagement over an extended period of time (there are no quick pathways to justice…this is long-term work!). It is important that you create the conditions that will support you to sustain your energy and enthusiasm to continue learning, applying your new knowledge, reflecting on what you are learning, and then adjusting your practices in continuous cycles of improvement. As you start on your personal journey of self-discovery and transformative learning, we offer a few suggestions that we believe are important for all adult learners to embrace before diving into a complex and emotionally sensitive professional learning experience:

- **Gender liberation is for everyone.** As adults, most of us have internalized constricting messages about what we can or cannot do based on our gender. The process of uncovering these messages and experimenting with recovering our "authentic gender self"—the self who moves through the world in ways that feel good rather than in ways that we think society expects of us based on our gender identity or attribution—can be a liberating and joyful experience! Whether or not you consider yourself gender expansive, the more you're able to connect with gender expressions that feel good to you—including gestures, patterns of movement, posture, cadence and pitch of voice, expression of emotion, activities you engage in, clothes you wear and other forms of style—the more you'll be able to model for your children what gender justice looks like.

- **Set a pace that works for you** and remember that the change you are striving for is long term. Think of yourself running a marathon and not participating in a short relay race. Allow yourself time and space to process what you are learning and integrate this emotional work into your practice piece by piece.

- **Find a colleague, buddy, or group to work through the book with.** As adults learn through social interaction, having one or more people to discuss the various ideas with will enhance your learning. Your buddy can also act as a critical friend—someone who can ask you clarifying questions about your beliefs and assumptions, and offer alternative perspectives and understandings without judgment. Working with others will also build in a process of accountability to help you maintain your commitment to continue learning about, discussing, and implementing gender justice practices in your classroom and program.

- **Identify allies who, like you, are committed to creating gender justice for young children.** Actively network and try to identify others who share your commitment and passion to create gender inclusive early childhood environments. Think of other colleagues and administrators you know, parents and family members, community organizations, local community members, groups online, and others who share your goals. Identifying a community to offer support and share stories with you will be energizing and will strengthen your ability to sustain your work.

- **Set reasonable goals for your learning and improvement.** Be kind to yourself and set yourself up for success! When you set goals for yourself, start small and realistic. Identify changes you can make and focus on those. Develop a way to document your slow and steady progress and take time to acknowledge and celebrate each and every "small win." Although you may envision grand changes, don't let perfect become the enemy of good! Small and actionable changes will add up and create a momentum that will be contagious and motivate you to keep going!

- **Identify roadblocks or barriers you imagine may create challenges for accomplishing your goals.** These could be your own internal barriers, external barriers (including structural, organizational/program), or cultural barriers. Name these barriers honestly and write them down to acknowledge them. Then, store them on your computer or file them away in a folder. Your focus will be to work on the changes you can make within your sphere of influence. Identify the barriers that are surmountable and those that are out of your reach or control.

- **Learn how to complete a body scan.** This involves pausing and paying attention to the clues our body gives us when we are experiencing stress. We all exhibit stress symptoms in different parts of our bodies. By learning to check in with yourself while you are working through this book, you can learn to identify when your body is signaling to you that you are feeling stress—

in your head, neck, jaws, hands, feet, hips, pelvis, lower or upper back, eyes, mouth, ears, stomach, or heart. If you do feel sensations of stress in your body, you can choose to engage in self-care activities to calm yourself down and stop your stress response system from activating. Try to stay in the learning zone and listen to your body's warnings that you are getting close to the danger zone.

- **Start a journal** to capture the range of feelings, questions, concerns, and achievements you make while you are on your gender justice learning journey.

- **Recognize that this is a long-term process.** Changes will not happen overnight for you or your programs: this is long-term work. Readers may want to return to this book many times as their knowledge, skills, and dispositions evolve. As you develop in your teaching practice, you will be ready to tackle additional layers of the transformative work we describe throughout the book. Return to this book often to see how far you have come and how much farther you can go.

- **Remind yourself why you are doing this challenging and essential work.** Sometimes when we are engaged in activities that are demanding, we need to stand up on a balcony and look down at the situations we are in to remind ourselves why we are working so hard by choice. Remind yourself that as an early childhood teacher, you are one of the most consequential people shaping and influencing children's lives. You have the power and responsibility to support every child to feel loved and cared for, valuable and visible, authentic and honest, and safe and protected. You also have the power and responsibility to choose attunement, connection, and responsiveness in a world that too often casts blame and creates shame. So, if ever your energy and perseverance start to fade, just remind yourself what brought you to this book in the first place and why you are motivated to do this work.

Building self-awareness through pausing: using reflection to interrupt gender inequitable practices

Building self-awareness begins by creating a "pause" to focus on our inner experience. Pausing allows teachers to think about, instead of act upon, our thoughts and feelings. By pausing to reflect, we strengthen our understanding of how our beliefs and feelings influence our interactions with others including the children, families, and staff we are working with on a daily basis (Steinberg & Kraemer, 2010). Reflection allows us to stop ourselves from reactivity, that is, the beliefs and behaviors we have automatically—including the words we say and the actions we are quick to take, especially in situations that are emotionally intense and stressful.

Through reflection, we create a "pause button" to "look back" and consider what we do automatically in our teaching practice, and think about why we make certain choices and who benefits and suffers, or is disadvantaged as a result. When we learn to reflect and systematically ask ourselves questions about who benefits and who is harmed or marginalized by a specific teaching practice, we open a door to discovering their taken-for-granted assumptions and the biases operating "under the surface," which may be unintentionally leading some children and families to lack safety, a sense of belonging, or the ability to learn and thrive in our care.

Shifting our understanding of gender and the way we socialize children to understand and relate to gender in our classrooms, programs, and early learning environments can only happen if we begin by turning inward to build self-awareness about our personal beliefs, assumptions, and lived experiences with gender across our lifespan. It is only when we teachers uncover our assumptions and beliefs that we can be in a position to thoughtfully consider what we hold as taken-for-granted "truths." We will likely need to interrupt some of these beliefs if we are going to work towards creating early childhood environments that foster social justice and gender equity.

What types of reflection questions can teachers begin asking themselves?

There are many questions teachers can use to begin their learning journey, and we encourage you to ask yourself questions that are the most authentic and meaningful for you. We provide some suggestions below and a longer, more comprehensive list in the Self-Study and Classroom

Audit Tool, which is included at the end of this chapter. Consider how you learn best before you explore the answers to these questions: Do you learn best through individual reflection? Through journaling? By thinking as you exercise, commute to work, or drink a hot cup of tea and sit quietly by yourself and think? Or do you think best when you are talking with others and identifying your thoughts and beliefs as you "think out loud" and have others ask you clarifying questions or simply respond to your ideas with their own stories and experiences? Choose the method of reflection that works best for you. The key is that you create a "pause" to ask yourself some questions and be open to "hearing" and learning about yourself.

BEGINNING REFLECTION QUESTIONS TO ASK YOURSELF

What is gender to me? Specifically:

— How did I learn about gender?

— How have gender norms limited my life (i.e., what your family, culture, and community communicated to you about what was expected of you related to gender)?

— How have gender norms benefited me?

— What gender assumptions and beliefs do I knowingly cling to?

— What do I love about my gender?

— How does my gender relate to, and interact with, the other social categories I identify with and belong to (e.g., race, ethnicity, socioeconomic status, sexual orientation, age, ability, religion, immigration status, etc.)?

— How does all this influence my work with young children?

— What feelings come up when I think about changing any of my beliefs about gender?

— What have been my historical responses to children breaking the rules of gender? Are there times when I've felt discomfort or even disgust?

- What fears do I hold about engaging in the work of gender justice in my program?

- How have my own beliefs about gender affected my teaching?

- How am I modeling my own gender with children? Is it in line with my authentic gender self?

Barbara Dray and Debora Wisneski (2011) developed a practice they call **"mindful reflection,"** a process that guides teachers to look inward and engage in deep reflection in order to identify their personal assumptions, biases, and deficit views and to replace them with practices that are more responsive and equitable. The motivation for this process is to support teachers to strengthen their sensitivity in working with a diverse student population, especially with children and families whose backgrounds are unfamiliar to the teacher (Harry & Klingner, 2006). Kendall (1996) calls for teachers to take the "emotional risk" of examining their deeply held beliefs that can affect how they treat children. She suggests that teachers use inward relection to listen and change how they respond to students who are different from them in some way (Dray & Wisneski, 2011, p. 29).

Dray and Wisneski (2011) also draw on the concept of mindfulness—the ability to be conscious about things we typically do automatically or unconsciously including our communication with others (p. 30)—as a process that can support teachers in order to interrupt their deficit-based beliefs, behaviors, and inequitable practices. Mindful reflection as a process supports teachers to move away from reactivity and to identify the attributions (or meanings they are automatically associating with the behavior of others). The authors explain that the goal of mindful reflection is to move away from "automatic pilot or mindless responses that are based on a person's own cultural frames of reference. Automatic pilot is the process in which a person is not conscious or aware of [their] responses to others" (p. 30). One way that teachers can learn to shift away from reactive—automatic pilot—thinking and behavior is to develop awareness about the attributions they ascribe to others:

A person who is aware of [their] attributions and takes time to reflect on them can minimize misattribution or misinterpretation of why someone behaves the way that [they] do... a person's cultural frame of reference or cultural background, as well as life experiences, guides how [they] respond to others. When a person's cultural background and/or life experiences are vastly different from those of people with whom [they are] interacting, there is a risk for a...misunderstanding...that can lead to conflict or misattribution... Therefore, teachers within diverse communities should become highly aware of their personal cultural background and lens for understanding behavior, as well as cultural norms or tendencies of others, so that they can reduce attributions that lead to prejudice, deficit thinking, and overgeneralizations. (Dray & Wisneski, 2011, p. 30)

How does mindful reflection work?

Dray and Wisneski describe a process with six steps that teachers can use to learn about their assumptions, beliefs, biases, and behaviors, and to use this information to interrupt inequitable teaching practices and become more attuned and responsive to the diverse children in their programs. The process of mindful reflection was originally designed to support teachers to become more culturally responsive in their practice. We have adapted Dray and Wisneski's original focus on culture to illustrate how the mindful reflection process can also be effective in supporting teachers to use reflection to become more responsive and attuned to gender diversity with young children.

While we expect those who are just learning about genders beyond the binary to use this tool to unearth biases about people who break gender norms, we have written it so that it can be used by anyone at any point in their gender journey. When some people start working towards supporting transgender children they will swing to the opposite end of the spectrum from traditional approaches, and begin discouraging all overtly gendered behaviors in children, even if those behaviors make those children happy and are not harming others. As you progress in your learning and growth, return to this tool from time to time and repeat the process, thinking of whichever child you are struggling to support at that time.

USING MINDFUL REFLECTION AT EVERY STAGE OF YOUR GENDER JOURNEY

The tool that follows will ask you to think of a child whose gender is challenging for you in some way. We expect that most readers will use this tool the first time to uncover biases and judgments about children and adults who break gender norms in ways that make them uncomfortable. This tool is designed to crack the surface of your underlying gender assumptions, attributions, and value judgments—factors that are influencing how you interact with and respond to children in your care. But it is also designed so that you can come back and repeat this exercise at any point along your gender justice journey, and so readers who come in with greater experience with gender expansiveness can still challenge themselves to uncover biases and assumptions.

This tool might be used to reflect on patriarchal inequities being played out in the classroom; as we've mentioned, gender bias is not equally distributed. Maybe there is a boy in the class who is exhibiting behavior that is aggressive, controlling, or disrespectful of others' bodily consent—patterns that mimic what is called toxic masculinity in adults (the limiting of male emotionality primarily to anger and dominance). This tool may be used to empathize with that child and think about how he might be hurting from the gendered expectations he is already trying to live up to, rather than ascribing anger and negative intentions to him.

Some teachers we've met, who are eager to start supporting all the TGE children in their care, have jumped all the way from an entrenched gender binary to trying to completely eradicate gender from their programs. A teacher in this mindset may use this tool while thinking of a presumed girl, who identifies as a girl and who loves pink and dresses and dolls and dancing and princesses—even if the teacher has removed as many of those things from the classroom as possible. They might reflect on whether or not a "gender-free" environment is supporting this girl's gender health and helping her feel seen.

A transgender teacher can use this tool as well, as nobody is immune from gender bias and attributions. Perhaps a transgender woman is struggling with how she can support one of the boys in her class when she sees him embody all the aspects of masculinity she felt were forced on her as a child. She might have to reflect on whether she thinks he shouldn't play sports all the time because it's what's best for him, or because she was forced to play sports against her wishes when she was young and those are painful memories for her. Maybe it's a little of both!

We hope you return to this tool each time you reach a new stage in your learning and you find you are struggling to support a child's gender for new reasons. There is no end to uncovering our assumptions, attributions, and biases!

Step 1: Identify the attributions you have about children's gender. Think about a child whose gender (identity, expression, pronouns, etc.) is challenging for you in some way. Ask yourself the following questions:

- Am I making assumptions about this child and their gender?

- Have I already judged this child's gender as being acceptable or unacceptable? Stop and describe what the child said or did that led you to the conclusions you have made.

- What leads me to believe that the child's gender is concerning or wrong? What is it about the child that is leading to my interpretation?

Step 2: Write out and reflect on your feelings and thoughts when you work with this child. Think about a specific interaction you have had with this child that involved your awareness of the child's gender identity/expression in some way. Write freely and describe what you can recall about the interaction. What happened? What was the child doing/ saying? How did you respond? Then read through your written reflection and ask yourself:

- What attributes am I assigning to the child? Have I made assumptions about this child's motivations, emotions, and intentions relating to their gendered behavior?

- How does this child make me feel? What thoughts went through my mind during this interaction?

- What are my worries or fears for this child? What are my worries or fears for other children in the class related to this child's gender? Can I identify specifically what it is I am afraid of or concerned could happen?

- Not knowing the best way to support the child?

- Not knowing the best way to support the rest of the children?

- Not knowing how to balance the two?

- Saying the wrong thing(s)?

- Having to facilitate challenging conversations with the children and families, or with my colleagues?

- Accidentally "outing" a child who has not shared their gender identity with others?

- Not "outing" a transgender child, and then facing community members who find out from someone else and are upset?

- Backlash either for acting or failing to act in a certain way?

• What might the impact of my fears be on this child in my care? Are there ways my own discomfort is limiting my ability to truly support and affirm the gender health of children?

• What are my assumptions? Why do I find the child's behavior problematic or concerning? Have I evaluated, interpreted, or judged their behavior?

Answering these questions will help you acknowledge your beliefs and assumptions about gender and help you notice whether you are using deficit thinking in the attributions you are associating with the child. Being honest with yourself about what you see may be difficult and lead you to experience some uncomfortable feelings. This is normal and a necessary part of transformative learning for teachers committed to becoming more equitable in their teaching practice. It is important that you not turn away from the process when you feel discomfort. If you find yourself nearing your danger zone of discomfort, take a break. Engage in self-care that is calming for you. Make a plan for reentering the process and staying in your learning zone.

The only way you will be able to discover any biases you have and to use this knowledge to help you improve your practice is if you are willing to begin with an honest acknowledgment of your authentic perspectives and to surface any prejudices you may have. Sensoy and DiAngelo (2017) describe prejudice as "prejudgment about members of social groups to which we don't belong based on limited knowledge or experience with the group. Simplistic judgments and assumptions are made and projected onto everyone from that group" (pp. 227–228). Prejudices prevent us from being effective teachers for every child.

Step 3: Consider alternative explanations by reviewing your documentation and reflections. This next part of the process supports us to more deeply examine the ways in which we are perceiving children and communicating with them, and then to rethink our initial interpretations. In order to do this, review your answers to the questions in Step 2, describing your interaction with the child. Reflect on the reasons this child may be doing what you observe them doing in your classroom (e.g., using a certain pronoun, wearing specific clothing, identifying with a gender different than their legal designation, engaging in aggressive masculinity, refusing to expand their gendered play choices, excluding others on the basis of gender). Consider how this child's behavior and choices are similar to or different from other children's behavior and choices in the classroom. Ask yourself:

- What are my expectations for the situation?

- How is this child meeting/not meeting my expectations?

- In what ways is this child's behavior supporting their learning and/or interfering with their learning? In what ways is this child's behavior supporting or interfering with other children's learning? Is there a type of learning happening that I previously have not seen or valued, but that is valuable to the child?

- Consider how the child's family responds to and interacts with this child and the messages they are communicating to the child about gender. What do I know about how they interact with the child at home?

Step 4: Check your assumptions. After you have reflected on the child's behavior and developed alternative explanations to expand or challenge your assumptions and surface your biases, it is helpful to identify individuals to act as critical friends who can help you further check your assumptions. For example, you might identify a colleague or friend you can share your reflections with and invite them to ask you probing questions and then provide you with their honest reactions to your ideas and to share their own perspectives. You might also consider identifying someone with expertise in gender diversity to share your reflections with, with their consent. Perhaps a professional who provides training or coaching on diversity (and ideally, gender diversity). It is also important to learn from the child's parents and family members about how they perceive their child's gender identity and expression, and the gender expectations and norms they hold and value in their family. After listening and learning from these conversations, teachers can ask themselves:

- Can I spend time sitting with, reflecting upon, and trying to understand why I have discomfort about children who embody gender in this way? What can I learn and unlearn from my discomfort?

- What are some alternative explanations or interpretations of the child's behavior that I had not considered previously?

Step 5: Make a plan; now it is time to ask yourself the following questions.

- How can I change or respond differently to this child?

- What can I do to reduce my own fears and anxieties prior to engaging with a child who makes me feel this way? If I am not able to prepare in advance, what can I do now to be attuned and responsive to the child so they feel safe, acknowledged, and supported in my care?

- What additional resources do I need to implement this change?

- What is one thing I can do daily to affirm this child's gender and support their gender health while I process through these feelings on my own?

- What is one thing I can commit to not doing anymore because it was a reaction that served to make me more comfortable, rather than to support the child?

After you have considered alternative explanations and developed a different interpretation of a situation, you will be able to change your behavior. You should develop a plan for making a change (e.g., a change in the way you communicate with this child, or a change in your classroom environment) and commit to trying it out.

Make a change and observe what happens as a result, and reflect on your reactions and feelings, as well as the child's/children's response.

Step 6: Continually Revisit This Process to Reassess Your Attributions and Your Progress in Being Responsive to Children. Learning to identify the attributions you associate with others, especially young children who are different from you, is challenging and long-term work. You will need to continuously reflect upon your relationships with children and honestly assess whether you are creating attuned, supportive, and caring relationships with every child. All teachers need to think about mindful reflection as a process that is ongoing. Remain committed to revisiting each step as needed as this will allow you to continue strengthening your ability to support all children to be successful in your classroom. (*Steps for Mindful Reflection and Communication to Strengthen Gender Inclusive Practices*, adapted from Dray & Wisneski, 2011.)

Scenario with Preschool Teacher Grace and two four-year-old children, Marcel and Sasha

Step 1: Explain the attributions that you (Teacher Grace) have about the child.

What did you observe? What happened? Marcel and Sasha playing together in the dramatic play area. Marcel was pretending that he was pregnant, and he said to Sasha, "I'm going to have three babies. I'm the mama!" Sasha looked confused and insisted that Marcel was a boy and could not have babies or be a mother. Marcel protested, "Yes, I can!" and he looked at me and said, "Sasha said I can't be a mother!" I looked over and said, "Marcel, Sasha is right. You can't be a mother. You are a boy and only girls can be mothers. Why don't you pretend to be a father in the family?"

How did the child react to your actions or comments? Sasha smiled and nodded her head up and down feeling acknowledged. Marcel started to cry and ran away. I found him in the corner of the room in a little ball, sobbing and saying to himself, "Yes I can be a mother. I don't want to be a father. No fair!"

Step 2: Write out or reflect on your feelings and thoughts when working with the child. Consider the potential for misinterpretations resulting from deficit thinking, prejudice, or overgeneralizations.

How does this child make you feel? What are your worries or fears? I feel uncomfortable when Marcel talks about wanting to be a mother. I worry because I don't know what to say in response. I also have fears that the other children might make fun of him or that my supervisor will get upset if she overheard Marcel and I don't interrupt this play.

What are your assumptions? Why do you find the child's behavior problematic? My assumptions are that there must be something wrong with Marcel if he wants to be a mother, because he is a boy. I find this behavior problematic because boys are supposed to think about becoming fathers when they grow up, and I want to protect Marcel because I care about him.

Step 3: Consider alternative explanations by reviewing your documentation and reflections.

Review the explanations and reflect on why the child may be doing what they are doing. Look for patterns in your behavior and the child's behavior. Marcel might be using play to explore gender identity or it might just be about exploring being pregnant and playing out the "mama" role. Or maybe Marcel knows that his gender identity does not match his legal designation at birth and he is trying to communicate this to a safe adult. I see in my observational notes that Marcel often takes on the role of females (mothers, sisters, princesses, etc.) in his play. I consistently discourage him from continuing with these roles.

What are your expectations for the situation? How is the student not meeting your expectations? In what way is the behavior interfering with learning? I have been expecting that Marcel's gender identity and expression would be determined by his anatomy, physiology, and legal designation at birth. Pretending to be a mother, sister, or princess in his play is not interfering with his learning.

What external factors and/or personal factors could be influencing the child's behavior? Marcel may not have opportunities to play at home. His family is often food- and housing-insecure, and they often move from one relative's house to another and sometimes have short stays in a local homeless shelter. Being at the childcare center may be the only place where he has time to engage in pretend play.

Step 4: Check your assumptions. Share your reflections with a colleague, parents, and/or community members. Meet with parents to learn more about expected and observed behaviors in the home.

Share your list of alternative explanations or interpretations of the child's behavior with a colleague, parents, and/or community members. I described my observations with a colleague who serves as a mentor for other early childhood teachers who want to learn about anti-bias education. I asked for her opinion about my reactions to Marcel. Should I be responding in a different way? She appreciated that I asked her opinion. She encouraged me to allow Marcel to have freedom in his play to explore and make discoveries about himself. She also loaned me a few books I could read and have available in the classroom. Finally, she gave me the name of a local organization that had some information I could read about TGE children and youth.

Meet with the family to learn more about their perspective in understanding the child. Do they notice the same behavior at home? Do they find it problematic? It's a bit challenging to speak with Marcel's parents because of all of the pressures they face on a daily basis, but I did ask Marcel's mom if she could find time to talk with me for a brief time. I explained that I wanted to learn more about Marcel and their family so I could be a supportive and responsive teacher. We had 15 minutes to check-in together recently and Priya, Marcel's mom, shared that Marcel likes to draw and play with his younger cousins when he is with his family. Sometimes he asks if he can try on her makeup. She doesn't mind and sometimes allows him to do so, and notices that it makes him happy. But this makes his father very upset so she has started telling him that he can't do so anymore.

Step 5: Make a plan.

How will you change or respond differently? I learned from my colleague that I should support Marcel to have the agency to choose the roles he wants to take in play, so I am going to try hard not to discourage and redirect him any longer. I am going to change my approach and, instead, work on listening to Marcel and taking seriously what he is communicating to me.

Brainstorm ideas on how to change the environment, your actions, and/or expectations for this child. I need to learn more about gender because these ideas are so new to me. I will add some new books into my classroom. My colleague said that she would be willing to come into my classroom to introduce a new persona doll who is gender expansive.

Experiment with responding differently. Note what happens. Reflect on your feelings as well as the child's response. Two weeks later, Marcel wanted to be the mother again while playing with Sasha. Sasha said he had to be the dad. This time, instead of agreeing with Sasha, I interrupted by saying: "Sasha, Marcel can be the mom if he wants. He gets to decide who he is, and you get to decide who you are." Then I remembered my colleague's advice to take an inquiry stance and asked, "Why did you say Marcel had to be the dad?" Sasha said, "Because you said boys can't be mothers!" I felt hot in the face at that! I took a deep breath and responded, "I did say that. But I was wrong. Now I'm learning about all the things that boys and girls and all kids can be for pretend and in real life too.

Consult with colleagues, parents, and/or community members while you experiment to check your assumptions and interpretations. I will continue to share what I am observing with my colleague and maybe ask her to come in and observe in my classroom independently.

Step 6: Continually revisit this process to reassess your attributions and your progress with the child.
Notice when you are overgeneralizing, attributing behavior within a deficit perspective, or behaving in prejudiced ways towards certain children. I want to learn how often and in what ways I am discouraging children from exploring gender, and/or attributing any behavior that diverges from traditional binary norms and expectations as problematic. I am going to start paying attention to my language more carefully and think about any fears I have about children and gender and whether my fears are based in deficit thinking.

Remember that this process is a continuous one, so revisit the steps periodically to continue your growth and understanding of children. Yes, there is a lot for me to learn about gender and creating a gender inclusive environment for young children. I look forward to using this process to keep learning and improving my teaching practice!

Be kind to yourself: your journey to gender justice will take you through different stages of building awareness and learning

One who knows not and knows not that they knows not is a fool; avoid them.

One who knows not and knows that they knows not is a student; teach them.

One who knows and knows not that they know is asleep; wake them.

One who knows and knows that they know is a wise person; follow them.

–Ancient proverb of multiple origins, adapted to be gender neutral

In 1969, Martin M. Broadwell described the path to becoming a good teacher as the "four levels of teaching" to show how teaching is a skill that can be developed and strengthened. These four levels were refined in 1974 by Noel Burch and described as the "four stages of learning any new skill." As we embark on any new learning journey, we will pass through at least some of these stages, and indeed the beginning of learning often signifies the beginning of Stage 2.

The first stage is "unconscious incompetence" in which we do not know what we do not know. We may be entirely unaware that there is a skill to learn, or we may inaccurately believe ourselves to be more competent than we are, but in the first stage we are not consciously aware of our deficit. For example:

- You might be misgendering a child without even knowing you are doing so.

- You might believe you "do not see gender" and that you treat all children the same, but your actions are subconsciously guided by assumptions and biases.

- You might have all the right intentions but be unaware that intention is typically not enough to create safety and justice for TGE children.

- You might not apply a "gender justice" lens to decision-making— "Oh, I love these new fairy figurines! I'll buy them for my class this year."—but not notice they are all female-coded with breasts and lipstick and long hair).

The second begins when we become aware of our lack of skill in an area. This is "conscious incompetence." In this stage we are willing to admit that we have learning to do. We make lots of mistakes, but we see it happening and can learn from them. Someone in Stage 2 might actively seek out help and resources to improve. In fact, there's a good chance you are in Stage 2 of learning about gender in early childhood just because you've picked up this book! However, maybe as you read you will discover some areas where you are still in Stage 1 or where you are already in Stage 3 or 4. During Stage 2, we work hard to practice and learn. We are conscious of our growth, and we put in a lot of effort to improve.

- Many teachers are tossed head first into Stage 2 when a transgender child joins their program or a child already in their care communicates that they are not the gender they were assigned. Teachers in this situation often want to support the child but realize they have no idea how.

- Lots of people spend a long time in Stage 2 when it comes to changing their language patterns—catching themselves addressing children as "boys and girls" or learning how to appropriately use all the terms we introduced earlier. It can take a long time to reshape our vocabulary!

- You might become aware of your need to apply a "gender-justice" lens. Following the example from above, you may buy the new fairy figurines, and then say, "Oops! I shouldn't have bought these. They are encoding a message that fairies are inherently feminine, and femininity looks a certain limited way."

Following is an example of a group of teachers in a childcare program moving from Stage 1 (unconscious incompetence) to Stage 2 (conscious incompetence):

As teachers we agreed we needed to shift the curriculum to be responsive to gender diversity, and that our first step would be to use inquiry to surface our own beliefs about gender. We talked about it at a couple of staff meetings and we asked each other, "What language do we want to use? How do we bring these children into our program and support them to feel safe and comfortable and a part of this environment?" By asking these questions and sharing our ideas together, we made important discoveries about the ways we were constraining young preschoolers' gender. We realized that at very early ages, we are putting kids into gender boxes. We are actually speaking to them differently! We talk to our young girls in really soft voices. As babies we call them "precious" and "beautiful" and "princess" and "delicate." Yet all the boys are hearing "Hey buddy," or "Hey tough guy." Although we had not realized it, the messages we were communicating to boys were reinforcing all the harmful and limiting stereotypes, "Boys shouldn't show emotion," "Boys don't cry," and "Boys play with trucks." It was ridiculous.
–Erika, Teacher, Child Care Center

Over time, our practice and hard work will lead us to Stage 3—"conscious competence." Here, we know what we are doing, and we are demonstrating competence. However, it still requires conscious effort to execute this skill.

- A teacher in Stage 3 might still keep a diary as they come up with new ideas for gender justice in their program, but the diary is already quite full and has undergone many revisions.

- Stage 3 might be where a transgender preschool teacher begins much of this work, because they've had life experience that made them much more consciously aware of these concepts from the start. They just have to intentionally incorporate them into their work with young children.

- You might purposefully apply your "gender justice lens" to decision-making: "Oh, I love these new fairy figurines! I'll buy them. Wait, let me check… do they show gender diversity? Do they show racial diversity? Different body shapes and sizes? Nope? I'll pass."

With enough practice and hard work, we may reach Stage 4—"unconscious competence." At this point, we are skilled enough that the task becomes routine or second nature. We no longer have to focus specifically on executing the skill to do it well. It's important to note, though, that reaching Stage 4 does not mean you're done learning! You may find that, just as you reach Stage 4 on one skill, the world of gender will be shifting and requiring a new skill or deeper understanding of you. The goal is not to ever finish learning, but to reach a stage of competence that makes new learning increasingly less scary or overwhelming.

- At this level, the idea of gender being open-ended and accessible for all children is woven into the fabric of your program's culture.

- You are comfortable and confident using language to discuss gender diversity both with children and with parents and peers. You no longer need a cheat sheet to get the terms right!

- You have shed many of your subconscious beliefs and biases that you discovered were harmful to gender justice. Now, when you spot a subconscious belief you didn't know you had, you are more curious than defensive, and you work to shape beliefs that move towards justice.

- You might automatically apply a "gender justice lens" to decision-making: "I'd love to buy a set of fairy figurines for my class, but it's hard to find diversity in these things. Maybe I'll put out some loose parts like acorns or stones with the little fairy tree house and see how the children use them."

Let's consider an example of a teacher moving through these different stages of learning about gender in early childhood. Imagine a child who starts using different pronouns than the ones assigned to them at birth. If a child who you have called "she" and "her" based on anatomy and legal designation comes to you saying "I'm a boy" and asks to be called "he" and "him," that signals your passing from unconscious incompetence to conscious incompetence. Prior to that conversation, you had been using "she" and "her" based on assumptions that are deeply ingrained in our society that gender is binary and determined by our anatomy. You were unconsciously using incorrect pronouns, but you had no idea they were incorrect until the child made you aware.

Now you are consciously incompetent. The first time you experience something like this it is unlikely that you will be able to easily switch pronouns. You will slip up, forget, and struggle. You may feel uncomfortable and fearful that you will make a mistake. It will take a lot of conscious effort on your part to practice using new pronouns, but eventually you will get it right more and more consistently. This is the area of conscious competence. Eventually, you will notice that you are using "he" and "him" all the time, and you have stopped having to think so hard or even think at all about doing it.

A parallel process occurs as you encounter more and more people (children and adults alike) who change their names and pronouns. You will find that with each person you meet, you will move through the stages more quickly, as you improve your skill in adapting your language to honor the gender identities of the people in your life.

Avoiding "the Big Freakout" (Payne & Smith, 2014): why it is so critical that teachers have accurate information about transgender and gender expansive people

Elizabeth Payne, Ph.D. and Melissa Smith, Ph.D. serve as the Director and Assistant Director of the Queering Education Research Institute (QuERI), respectively. In 2014, they released the findings of a study they conducted interviewing district-level administrators, principals, teachers, and student support professionals from five elementary schools. Each participant had a transgender student they were working to support. Payne and Smith sought to understand teacher experiences and responses to working with transgender children at the elementary school level.

The researchers found that **fear and anxiety are common responses** from teachers when they have a transgender student in their classroom. This fear and anxiety limits their ability to support and affirm TGE children.

Some teachers had concerns for the other children in the classroom with underlying beliefs that **transgender bodies were "threatening."** These teachers felt that other students and parents had a "right to know that a 'gender transgressor' was in their midst" even if the TGE child did not want peers and adults to know about their gender identity.

Most teachers expressed **feeling unprepared professionally** to understand and support LGBTQI+ students. When training resources do exist, they largely omit or misrepresent TGE identities, and/or come from a deficit model (e.g., TGE children are "at-risk" and need counseling, and likely to attempt suicide).

Teachers who wished to affirm transgender children **feared backlash** from parents, administrators, co-workers, and even within the larger community teachers also expressed **concerns over the lack of policies and procedures** specific to TGE children and families at their school.

The authors concluded that without having accurate information about gender diversity, and specifically transgender identity, teachers perceived the presence of a transgender child as a "crisis" that threatened the safety of a school environment. It goes without saying that treating any child as a threat to a school community would be traumatic for the child and their family and would communicate harmful messages about diversity, respect, and inclusion to all children and adults in the school community.

What are the implications of this study for you as an early childhood teacher?

Research focused on early childhood environments has documented some of the same themes. For example, Unger (2015) found that early childhood teachers reported having no literature or resources to guide them in supporting gender expansive children:

> Adam, a preschool teacher in Northern California working with a gender expansive three-year-old child, expressed feeling confused and adrift as he began to grasp the child's gender expansiveness: "I felt like I was in the dark and just grasping at straws trying to figure shit out. I was just like, 'I'm totally lost. I don't know what I am doing. I'm swimming upstream.'"

You can play a critical role in stopping teachers you work with from panicking and inadvertently teaching children that they are a threat or that they are to be feared.

How can you advocate for your school, center, or programs to seek out resources on TGE children and families?

We all need to affirm and empower children as early as possible so they can be resilient in the face of anyone who fears their presence, as they will unfortunately experience discrimination in our current cultural climate.

Where in your program's policies and practices are you reinforcing the gender binary?
How can you revise them to communicate about the natural gender diversity that exists in people?

Do you have relationships with transgender people in your life? If not, are there ways you could commit to learning about and making personal connections with transgender people?
Payne and Smith's (2014) research indicates that having personal relationships with transgender adults might be a significant factor in increasing educators' comfort and confidence in working with transgender children. If you don't know any transgender adults personally, try following transgender folks on YouTube or watching affirming and empowering documentaries about transgender and gender expansive individuals.

Learning to manage resistance in yourself and others

As you do this work, you will likely encounter resistance—active and passive, internal and external, conscious and subconscious. Our culture has been drenched in binary notions of gender and deeply ingrained stereotypes, expectations, and roles (based on a concept of gender that is strictly defined by anatomy) for so long that opening the doors to new narratives and conceptions of gender will most certainly cause discomfort around and within you. Some of the forms of resistance can be foreseen and planned for in advance.

José Medina (2013) describes various ways we often resist ideas, conversations, and work that highlights oppression and the perspectives of the oppressed. When individuals live their whole lives as a member of a dominant social group, they often develop a sense that they are confident in knowing how the world works, because their own experiences have always been validated and normalized by the dominant culture. When confronted with perspectives that are different from their own, individuals may find that they don't feel a need or desire to learn about them. And some people, often the ones who benefit the most from the dominant cultural beliefs and norms in place, actively work against having alternative perspectives voiced and discussed openly.

What does resistance look like in practice? A very common form of resistance is seen when an administrator flatly refuses to believe that young children are capable of understanding their own gender well enough to identify differently from the gender designation they were given at birth. Another form is seen when a co-teacher casually dismisses a teacher's concerns about a child's apparent gender-related distress by saying, "I'm sure it's nothing. She's just a tomboy. Stop making a big deal out of it." Resistance is at play when someone observes you greeting your class in the morning and notes that you seem to speak softer to the girls and comment on their clothes, while being exuberant with the boys and asking about their activities the night before, and you respond by saying "I treat all my children equally, regardless of their gender!" You are resisting their message because you want to believe that you are unaffected by gender stereotyping. When faced with evidence that contradicts our desires, we have many ways of resisting the truth in order to make ourselves feel better in the moment.

What can you do to manage resistance when it arises? All forms of resistance are predictable, and they can each be addressed when you know how to spot them. First, teachers can respond to resistance by **modeling the importance of humility**. We must all practice reminding ourselves regularly that our own experiences are not universal, that they are not more true or valid than someone else's just because they are ours. We can help each other remember this in ways that are caring yet firm when we encounter resistance from others. Second, teachers can reduce the impact of resistance by **asking questions and developing a learning stance**. If you try hard to come from a place of interest and curiosity in all your interactions with children, you can shift yourself and others away from being resistant to change by simply using reflection questions to guide your practice. Notice when you have a strong emotional reaction to something. Take that experience and turn it into reflection questions; for example: What assumption about gender did I have in that interaction? What did the child just communicate to me and what did I communicate back in my response? Turning our reactive moments into questions we can explore helps teachers develop a learning stance, and this will guide them to develop conscious competence.

It is our assumption that early childhood teachers come to work with the intention of supporting all children to learn and grow. It is very difficult for any teacher to think that their beliefs, actions, or words might be causing harm to a child. Sometimes it's easier to disregard information and perspectives that point to this as a possibility than it is to sit with the uncomfortable feelings this knowledge creates and to change our ways for the benefit of the children. Tackling closed-mindedness requires open-mindedness, but this is much more easily said than done. Open-mindedness (in ourselves and others) is uncomfortable. It's hard, never-ending work to constantly make ourselves better. It has very little solid ground and doesn't stay still for long. It requires us to **try unfamiliar things, allow ourself to make mistakes, and to learn from them.** But it's also exciting! Being open-minded allows us to learn about as many ways of living and being as there are people alive. Being humble about our own limits in knowledge and understanding of others is also one of the very best ways to understand ourselves better.

Working against resistance can be exhilarating and satisfying. It can also be draining and may feel like an uphill battle especially in an environment with few supports. We encourage everyone to **make room for self-care.** We encourage you to return to the beginning of this chapter and choose a few strategies that will help you sustain your energy and enthusiasm to continue on this journey. And remember, you may not need to address every time a co-worker makes a mistake if they are moving in the right direction in the long run. Have compassion for your own and others' learning journeys. Remember that these kinds of shifts don't happen overnight.

Self-study and classroom audit tool: self-work

Use the questions below as a guide to reflect on your own gender identity, expression, and learning journey (questions 1-6) and your beliefs, expectations, and understandings about gender more generally (questions 7-14). Finally, consider what value you place on doing work towards gender justice and what steps you will take towards personal accountability (questions 15-18). If you think your answer to any of the self-work questions is "This doesn't apply to me," we encourage you to dig a little deeper!

1. What do I love about my gender?

2. When was a time I felt really affirmed or experienced a sense of belonging in my gender?

3. What are some obstacles I've faced in trying to authentically express and represent myself?

4. What are some ways that others have forced me to fit into their beliefs and expectations about gender?

5. What are some ways society's gender norms have limited me or hurt me?

6. Has there been a time when I felt a disconnection between how someone saw my gender and who I know myself to be?

7. What are some ways I've forced others to fit into my beliefs and expectations about gender throughout my life?

8. What are some conscious and subconscious reactions I have when my expectations about gender are disrupted?

9. Which of society's expectations about gender have always felt easy and natural for me to go along with, without questioning?

10. Am I willing to lean into and sit with feelings of discomfort when my beliefs and expectations about gender are disrupted?

11. Am I willing to approach those who challenge my beliefs, values, and concepts of gender with curiosity rather than judgment?

12. When I listen, am I open to being affected or changed?

13. Do I believe that each child in my care is the expert on their own gender, and am I ready to follow their lead and to support them in their journey?

14. What are some aspects of my gender expression, behavior, identity, and journey that break gender norms? How can I highlight these in my program as strengths?

15. How do I and my students benefit from understanding gender diversity, confronting stereotypes, and knowing ourselves? How does this impact cisgender as well as transgender and gender expansive students?

16. Who can I ask to be a buddy/accountability partner to support me in this work, if I don't already have one?

17. How will I continue my learning about gender, including seeking out a diversity of first-person perspectives about gender?

18. What are some language habits I will work on changing? Acknowledging that it is very difficult to change language patterns I've used my whole life –but knowing that it's for the health of the children in my care–how will I practice these changes?

—— Chapter 4 ——

Co-Creating Dynamic Gender Justice Curricula and Early Childhood Environments

Emma is Lucien's best friend, and they play "Sisters" every day. They play this so often, in fact, that Emma refers to Lucien as "she" even when they are not playing "Sisters." Soon other children do, too. One day Lucien is eating lunch and observes: "Look! It's all girls at this table, and all boys at that table!"

Sadie frowns and says, "You are not a girl."

Lucien is quiet for a moment and says, "I am a girl." Emma quickly repeats, "Lucien IS a girl." The room is quiet and most of the children are listening, curious.

Sadie starts to cry, insisting, "YOU ARE A BOY! LUCIEN IS A BOY!" Lucien also starts to cry. "Stop saying that!"

Teacher Heather asks both children to come outside with her for a moment, to talk. Heather is worried for Lucien. "Sadie," Heather says, trying to keep her voice kind and even, "If Lucien says she's a girl, why do you say she isn't? Why do you think she's a boy?" Sadie is sobbing now. "I don't know! But Lucien is a boy! He is!" Heather sees how confused and distressed Sadie is. She takes a deep breath and asks Sadie if she would like a hug.

Lucien is already curled into Heather's lap, no longer crying, but frowning and breathing hard. Sadie nods and moves in close, looking worriedly at Lucien. Heather notices this and asks, "Do you want to ask Lucien something?" Sadie pouts and nods. "I want to ask Lucien why he says he is a girl, but he wears Star Wars and also Teacher Meg calls him a boy."

It's true. Teacher Meg does sometimes have the children line up boy-girl-boy-girl, and Lucien is always called for "boy." Heather understands *why Sadie is confused. Lucien responds, "Because I am a girl. Maybe sometimes I'm a boy, but mostly I'm a girl, and I don't want you to call me a boy. Don't call me a boy, Sadie!" Sadie frowns, but doesn't say anything. Heather asks Sadie if she would like it if someone insisted that she is a boy, when she feels like a girl. She replies that she would not like that. Heather asks Lucien if she wants to say anything else to Sadie, and Lucien shakes her head. The teacher brings both children inside, and they quietly finish lunch.*

Depending on your training, you may be thinking, "What does this story have to do with curriculum?" To many people, curriculum means teacher-led activities, projects, worksheets, and circle-time agendas. Others have argued that in early childhood education we need a broader view of curriculum that recognizes that:

- Children learn primarily by doing, second by what adults are modeling, and much less by what adults tell them.

- Curriculum includes children's everyday moments of play and interaction (CDE, 2016). Children don't stop learning when circle or project time is over. Children are learning during all times of the day including playtime, snack time, and when they are using the toilet.

- Curriculum is co-created by children as they bring their whole selves including their unique styles and interests, family culture and social identities, biases, temperaments, actions, thoughts, and ideas into our programs.

- A comprehensive definition of curriculum includes: "the play spaces designed as environments for learning, the care routines designed to invite children's active participation, and the interactions and conversations with children that support their understanding of themselves and others" (CDE, 2016, p. 25).

As the story above shows, children's understandings of gender and such key gender questions as "How do you know what a person's gender is?" are forming and being negotiated all the time, not just at circle time. As teachers, we are constantly required to be "on" in our readiness to help children navigate the often emotional moments of conflict, as well as moments of self-exploration and trust that come up throughout the day. While in the presence of children, we are always teaching. Even if we don't think we are teaching, we are teaching unconsciously by communicating to children how to organize their understanding of the world, the ideas we do/do not value, and the expectations we have for children's participation in the classroom and larger community. We will return to this story about Sadie and Lucien throughout the chapter as we discuss how gender concepts are "taught" and "learned" through curriculum, which includes language, interactions, transitions, routines, environments, and play, as well as teacher-led activities, projects, and circle times.

This is a lot of ground to cover in one chapter, and any one of those subjects could have its own book! We hope to leave you with a few ideas of starting points as you apply what you have been learning to your own program curriculum. We begin by looking at strategies and ideas for teaching young children about gender agency and diversity. We then delve into issues around gender bias and how we can teach children to advocate for themselves and others.

Supporting children's gender awareness and exploration of gender identity and gender expression through curriculum

We need to teach young children that adults value their right to have gender agency. This supports every child to develop self-pride without being limited by constraining gender roles and norms. As we support children's gender agency, we also communicate messages about the value of gender diversity.

Just because you don't look like a gender but you actually are, it doesn't mean that you can't go in [the bathroom of your choosing]. Because you're the one that decides. –Alex, age 8

A brief recap: What is gender agency and how do teachers support it with young children? As previously discussed, child agency is the ability for children to act independently and participate in decisions that impact their lives. When we support children's gender agency, we acknowledge their ability to determine and communicate about their gender identity (what they know themselves to be inside) and to explore gender identity options beyond the gender assigned to them at birth. Further, when teachers support children's gender agency, they listen to what children communicate to them about their gender, and they respond with caring, attuned, and responsive interactions. Specifically, they use verbal and nonverbal signals that reinforce messages of welcome, acknowledgment, and respect to all children, including and especially those who may not feel the gender label assigned to them at birth is an accurate description of who they know themselves to be.

Yet, teachers have an additional responsibility with very young children. In order for infants, toddlers, and preschoolers to develop gender agency, they first need language, pictures, and stories that offer ideas about who is it possible for them to be and to become—"I'm a boy!" "I'm an in-betweener!" "People can change their gender!" "I don't have to choose!" It is only when children are exposed to vocabulary and ideas that help them authentically name their thoughts, feelings, and experiences related to gender, that we support them to be able to honestly tell us who they are. If adults offer only limited language and ideas about gender, young children will learn early on that who they are is not acknowledged by the adults around them, and this leads to hiding and feelings of shame.

Maybe it's a phase. Maybe it's not a phase, it's just pretend. And maybe she's nonbinary. Those are all options. We came through with a plan for each possibility—what we could do that would be affirming right now and also take care of this possibility. We'll keep paying attention to her gender and what's working for her, and be willing to change that if it changes. Because one thing the staff were hesitant around was "What if she's not really trans and we call her this?", and then that's bad because later she doesn't want that. The answer is: Well, if later she doesn't want that, we can change it again. That made people feel better.

We can't just wait to see what the kids are gonna show us, because they've already read our values and are going to be reflecting them back to us. So, this whole idea that you can be objective and wait and see: I don't think that's real. I would like to proactively stack the deck with many options, and maybe there's a kid who would be really feminine if they were exposed to it. It's not really fair to wait and see, and make them find out the hard way. -Toby, former Infant-toddler and Preschool Teacher

I want to support children's gender agency but I have no idea how to begin. Where do I start?

It is important to communicate respect for people of all genders and family structures right away through the wording on your intake/enrollment forms.

- **Allow for multiple primary caregivers and allow them to write in their own caregiving roles** (such as "Grandpa" or "Maddy," a mash-up of "Mom" and "Daddy" used by transgender author Jennifer Finney Boylan. Other examples of non-binary parental terms include Baba, Poppy, Pare, and Momo.[13]

- **Allow family members to write in their child's gender** rather than pick between female and male.

Start with the children and families who are in your classroom or program. Invite children and adults in your classroom to share words they use for their own genders and the genders of their family members (as well as many other aspects of their personal and social identities, family structures, etc.), through a mixture of large-group, small-group, and one-on-one conversations. As you build a group vocabulary around who is in your classroom, underscore the basic anti-bias message: We are all similar and we are all different, and aren't those differences wonderful? Model for children and families your value for supporting gender agency and making gender diversity visible in your classroom. The following are several strategies to get you started:

- **Reinforce gender agency with introductions.** Model gender agency when you introduce yourself: "I like to be called 'he' and 'she.' What do you like to be called?" Introducing other adults is another opportunity to use language that communicates to children that gender agency is valued by the adults in their classroom. When you are introducing someone and you do not know what pronoun(s) they use, you could say: "This is our new guest teacher, Vivian. Vivian, what pronouns do you use? I like to be called "he" and "she."

- **When talking about people who you don't know the gender identity of, use language that avoids assigning them a gender.** Instead of "that girl," "that kid," or "that person," try saying, "I don't know what their gender is—we'd have to ask them!"

Try saying "your baby" or "your little one" instead of "your son/daughter" or "Is it a boy or a girl?"

Are you having a boy or a girl?

Adults' curiosity and insistence on categorizing a child's gender begins from the earliest moments of their young lives. We all know that one of the most common questions following the announcement of a pregnancy or adoption is "Are you having/adopting a boy or a girl?" To many, learning the answer to this question feels like an entitlement and a right, and some adults even get angry when parents choose not to discuss their child's gender or opt not to answer this question definitively.

Many individuals believe that they must know a child's gender (and it can only be male or female) to know how to relate to them: what clothes and gifts to purchase for them, how to talk about and prepare for their presence, and how to dream and imagine their future lives and roles within the family and community. Making these sweeping assumptions about a child's life (and demands of parents!) before they are even born, or before they join a forever family, is unfair to that child. It removes the child's agency to build their own unique gender. It is also unfair to the family, who may not want to make these kinds of assumptions about their child.

We must shift our attitudes, beliefs, and behaviors towards an approach that emphasizes our commitment and responsibility to **a child's agency even before they are born**. Let's see what it looks like in practice to disrupt these cultural patterns and shift towards a more child-centered approach...

How can early childhood teachers support a child's gender agency even before birth?

You can show genuine interest, care, or concern for someone who is pregnant or in the process of adopting a child without asking about gender. There are many other questions that you can ask to communicate your investment and interest in their lives. You might say, "How are you feeling?" or "Can I organize meals to be delivered to your family for the first few weeks after your baby/child comes home?" If you notice a pregnant person or adoptive parent looking uncomfortable when they are asked about the gender of their child, you can ask, "Would you like support responding to that question?"

Some ways to diffuse questions about the genders of children who have not yet arrived might include:

- "Well, we don't know yet, but when the child tells us, we'll let you know!"

- "My baby probably won't care what color clothes they wear for a while, but if you're gift shopping, I could really use one of those nursing wraps! I like earth tones."

- "We're having a kid! We don't want them to be treated one way or another based only on their body."

- **Use language that is inclusive of diverse family structures.** Instead of "We're going to go around and talk about our moms and dads," you could state, "We're going to go around and talk about who's in our family." Notice when you are using language which communicates to children that heteronormative families are valued as the "norm." To become gender inclusive, this language should be replaced with words and ideas that reinforce for children that there are many types of families (with family members of different genders), and all of them are welcomed, respected, and valued in the classroom community.

- **Use the words that staff, children, and families use for themselves to build your classroom vocabulary around gender.** Words have more meaning when they are associated with a real person. Ask children and family members how they like to be talked about including pronouns and gender identity words like "girl" or "in-betweener" or "boy." Following is an example of one preschool program that has adopted this practice:

At one preschool, for years, a gender expansive teacher, Crane, described herself as "part girl, part boy," whenever children asked about his gender (the teacher uses a mix of "he" and "she" pronouns). One year a transgender parent, Jay, introduced himself as an "in-betweener." The teacher adopted this word after hearing it and began to use it with the children. This term became a part of the classroom culture that has endured over time. Over the years, some children have claimed an in-betweener identity themselves. Others have incorporated it into their worldview, as shown by one child who was setting places at a table during play: "Here's where Mr. Nobody sits, and here's where Mrs. Nobody sits, and here's where in-betweener Nobody sits!" When another teacher at this school site recently asked the children for the gender words they use for themselves, they generated several additional words that have since become incorporated into the current classroom culture— including "boy-girl," "everything," "witch," and "spider."

- **Do not shy away from talking about body parts including genitals. Children learn important messages about gender agency by the way adults talk about anatomy and physiology on a daily basis.** When conversations about anatomy come up between children, offer clarifying, affirming information without shutting down or shaming children's curiosity. Explain that body parts don't dictate gender. It is critical for children's safety to be able to name and talk about their own genitals. When we shy away from talking about these body parts, we fail to give children the language they need to tell us when something's wrong— from a rash to inappropriate touches. We also can communicate shame and stigma that can lead to insecurity, anxiety, and a host of problems as their sexuality develops down the line.

Most child development experts recommend using scientific and clinical terms for body parts, such as "vulva," "penis," "vagina," and "scrotum." These terms come from a Western medical tradition that positions itself as accurate, objective, and neutral, and casts locally or personally used terms (such as "pee pee" or "'gina") as immature and inferior. However, Western science and its terminology are not neutral; they are tied to white, upper-class, patriarchal, and cisgender morality and social norms. TGE and intersex people have a long history of being pathologized and oppressed by the medical establishment and its language, which names our body parts for us without our consent. We believe that there is nothing inherently harmful about using non-medical terms for body parts. *Which* words we use are less important than how we use them—*respectfully* (respecting the child's agency and the language they feel comfortable using for themself), *matter of factly* (without comedy, euphemism, or shaming), and *specifically* so that children have the language for their own bodies and can tell us when something is wrong. A teacher might explain:

> We all have body parts called genitals. Genitals are what our urine comes out of and we use them for other things later in life. Some people have genitals that look like a tube with a bag underneath. The science words for these are penis and scrotum, but people use many other words for them. Some people have genitals that look like a slit with a little mound at the top. The science word for this is vulva, and the vagina is the inside part, but people use many words for them as well. No two people's genitals look exactly alike! Genitals are a special part of your body and it's important to keep them safe.

In the following quote, a teacher describes working with a three-year-old TGE child who has clear ideas about their own genitals:

> Adi says that they have a penis now, and, you know, pees at the tree, and some of the older kids are questioning and challenging that they don't have a penis, that they have a vagina. And we're like, "Actually, Adi knows exactly what sex they have, and Adi is able to decide whether they have a penis or a vagina or not." And it's also just a good example to show you that children know who they are as soon as they're born. And it's important that we foster that with our curriculum and our daily routine. –Avé, Infant-toddler and Preschool Teacher

Another teacher describes the tension between wanting to respect children's agency and needing language to describe their genitals:

> That's something I think I'm still studying, especially as I identify as intersex. So how we're talking about the body with children, and what we're naming things—I don't actually feel comfortable with what I'm doing right now, naming a penis a penis, or whatever... I want them to be able to have their own names and their own autonomy in what they call their body parts. And as a teacher, I'm like, "I need your penis to be pointing down at the toilet 'cause I'm not trying to have urine all over the place." –Mitali, Infant-toddler and Preschool Teacher

This same teacher describes a strategy of asking based on the concept of consent (i.e., giving permission for something to happen): "Can I call this your penis?" or "What do you call this?" or "Is it okay that I say…?"

The bottom line with terminology is: "If there's something wrong can I identify it?" Children need language to tell us when something's not right, whether it's a rash or someone touching them inappropriately. For example, I've heard teachers use the word "bottom" to mean everything below the waist and above the knees; but then if a child says, "So and so touched my bottom," there's a range of what that could mean, and it's not necessarily setting off alarm bells. –Lydia, Early Childhood Sexual Health Consultant

Using gender inclusive language to talk about children's body parts during diapering and toileting routines

"Jiro, I'm going to pull your underwear up over your penis now. I usually call that a penis–do you have a different word you use? 'Wee wee'? That's a nickname a lot of people use. The science word is 'penis.' Are you okay with me calling it a penis?"

"Yes, Sandy, your urine is coming through a small hole near the top of your–I usually call that a vulva. Does that sound okay to you?"

"Gemmy, I'm going to wipe your vulva now. The cloth feels cool! When you get older, you can tell me the words you use for your own parts."

———

Leah (age 4): "Sadie is a girl because she has a vagina, right?"

Teacher: "Sadie is a girl, and she does have a vagina! But a person decides if they are a boy or a girl or both or neither, based on how they feel, not by what body parts they have."

What if everyone in my classroom is cisgender?

Always presume there are TGE people in your class and community. They may be hiding or not fully aware of their genders yet. They may be cisgender now, and have been TGE in the past or will be TGE in the future. The following strategies apply to classrooms where everyone appears cisgender for now, as well as classrooms that include currently "out" TGE people.

Introduce the word "cisgender." It is important that you name and identify identities that are privileged in society like heterosexual partnerships and cisgender identities, rather than only talking about "other" identities like LGBTQI+ and lifestyles as examples of diversity. This can be done throughout the day and embedded within your curriculum. For example, you might begin a story: "Once upon a time there was a girl named Ronja. Ronja was a cisgender girl. That means that when she was born, grown-ups guessed she was a girl, and when she got old enough to decide for herself, she said, 'Yep! I'm a girl! They guessed right.' Now Ronja lived in the middle of a forest…"

Highlight the diversity of gender expressions (including hair and clothing style choices), interests, skills, and roles among people with cisgender identities in your program. It's important that cisgender teachers and adults talk with children about their gender identities, expressions, and anatomy and physiology, and how they are treated in the world based on their genders. When we don't, we reinscribe that we are "normal" and that gender is an issue only for people who break that norm. A TGE teacher explains:

I do think it made a difference to have people, kids, hear about my own gender and my own body. I think what made it uncomfortable was that they were hyper-focused on just me. Whereas if more teachers, even cis teachers, were comfortable talking about their bodies, that could have diffused that focus. [The workplace culture] needs to be very body positive to be trans positive, or to be gender positive in general. –Toby, former Infant-toddler and Preschool Teacher

Cisgender teachers can share different aspects of their own gender stories with children. Here are some examples from cisgender teachers:

For a long time I didn't wear dresses because people told me it would be hard to move around and play in dresses. But then I realized, "I love wearing dresses! They make me feel glamorous and comfortable." And I discovered that lots of kinds of dresses are super-easy to move around in, and I can do all sorts of things in a dress.

One teacher who works with 3–5-year-olds explains:

I want to show the children I work with that nobody fits within all the gender norms and expectations, but I don't want it to be forced or to come off as a joke. I think I'm going to tell them about the experiences I had as a boy who always loved to dance and act. I was bullied for it as a child, but I'm proud of who I am and the things I love. I fit a lot of the norms of adult malehood, but I still love to dance and put on costumes for dramatic play!

Another teacher who works with infants and toddlers says:

Taking out my tools and fixing things as a female provider, I can see children look at me and have gears turn. I also love getting in the mud and getting dirty! —Jess, Family Care Provider

Bring more gender diversity into your program/classroom! There are many ways you can do this. Here are just a few to get you started:

- **Invite guests of all genders, including TGE genders, into your program.** Remember that "diversity" means all different genders, including cisgenders. Make sure that you have a wide gender representation among the guests who come into the classroom. When bringing in a TGE person to interview, make sure not to "other" them; acknowledge that their gender is one part of them and not the primary reason they are being invited into the classroom. For example, you might invite a firefighter into the classroom who happens to be a trans woman. During the conversation, the firefighter describes different parts of her identity. Her gender is named but not the main focus of her presentation or of the children's discussion. This "normalizes" the diversity of genders and avoids "othering" genders outside the binary by treating them as "exceptional" or diverging from a cisgender "norm." Below is an example of this taking place with a nonbinary dancer who was invited into a preschool classroom as a guest:

I invited my friend who was a dancer to my preschool classroom to lead movement activities with the kids. We did not plan to talk about gender, but when I introduced my friend, I used they/ them pronouns. When it was time for questions, the children were curious about why I was saying "they," so my friend explained about being nonbinary: "I don't feel like just a boy or just a girl." This explanation made an impression and months later the children were asking, "When is your friend coming back? The one who's called 'they'?" –Encian, Preschool Teacher

Again here, the guest's gender was not the focus of their presentation— the focus was leading dance and movement activities. But their gender was part of their whole self, and it came into the conversation as the children were curious about an unfamiliar pronoun.

- **Practice normalizing gender expansiveness by sharing narratives of transgender and gender expansive people that are not centered on struggle or "othering."** For example, a teacher might narrate:

  Once upon a time there was a boy named Tani who lived with his mama. Tani loved finger-painting and climbing on rocks and making necklaces. Tani had a body that made grown-ups guess he was a girl when he was born. But when he got older he told his mama, "You got it wrong! I'm a boy." Now one day Tani was out climbing on rocks at the park, when...

  A family care provider who identifies as a cisgender woman relates this story: The other day Corinne was sitting in my lap, and said to me, "You have spikes (chin hairs) just like my pa and grandpa!" I responded, "You're right, I do have some whiskers there." Later I relayed this to Corinne's dad, who was mortified. I told him I think it's important for kids to see that femininity doesn't always look the same way. The dad replied: "Oh yeah, I guess that is good."

- **Also consider bringing your students out of the classroom and into the community!** Encourage children to notice things about people they see or meet, and discuss their observations with the class. Remind them to ask for consent before asking personal questions of people, especially strangers. "Can I ask you about your gender?" or "Can I ask you about your hair?" are respectful questions. Opening with "Are you a boy or a girl?" or "Why is your hair like that?" is not respectful. Explain that not everyone wants to talk about their gender, and it can feel rude to them.

On our trip to the park, we saw a person with punk-style hair and clothes. Some of the children were asking, "Is that a boy or a girl?" I told them, "I don't know that person's gender. Can we ever tell a person's gender just by looking?" It opened up a conversation. We talked about clues like hairstyle and clothing style, but also talked about examples of people who don't fit the clues—like boys who wear dresses and girls with shaved heads. I asked, "Is everyone either a boy or a girl?" and that started a conversation too. In this case, the kids didn't end up talking with the punk, but later at circle time we practiced respectful ways of asking personal questions for next time. –Maria Luis, Preschool Teacher

If age-appropriate TGE-centered events are happening in your area, share the details with families in your program. Examples are Drag Queen Story Hour, or family areas at Pride celebrations. Explain to families why it's important for children to meet people of diverse gender identities and expressions. (Note: Check whether events are open to everyone or if they are specifically for families with TGE members.)

Arrange your classroom environment and introduce curriculum that communicates your support and respect for gender diversity. The following are a few of the many ways you can send signals to children that your environment is a safe and inclusive space that values gender diversity.

- Place **"All Gender" signs on your bathrooms** to reinforce gender inclusivity instead of segregating bathrooms and toilets by gender. We recommend a sign that simply has a picture of a toilet.

- **Organize your cubbies alphabetically instead of by gender.**

- **Label extra clothes bins by type of clothing rather than by gender.** Extra clothes bins are a common item in early childhood classrooms for all the moments when children need to change an item of their clothing. Maybe a child gets muddy while playing outside or soils themself before making it to the toilet, or gets wet while playing at the water table. There are many reasons why teachers keep extra clothing in their classrooms. This clothing is distinct from "dress-up" as extra clothes bins are for "real-life" use, not for pretend play. However, the same choices should be made available to children with extra clothes bins. Specifically, categories should not be separated into traditional male- and female-coded clothing and offered to children in this restricted manner (e.g., only offering male children clothing from the "boys" extra clothes bin). Instead, organize clothing by type— onesies, pants, shirts, warm stuff—but include traditionally coded male and female options for each type of clothing: e.g., "Extra clothes are in the large bin under the cubbies. Zoë can choose from that bin." The opening vignette for this book reflects how important this small change can be for a TGE child.

"No Such Thing as Girl Clothes": The caption of this illustration reads, "You can't put clothes into groups of girl clothes or boy clothes! Just wear what you want to wear." The figure on the right says, "You're a boy! Don't wear a dress." The figure on the left replies, "No such thing as girl clothes." Credit line: Chicken.

- **Recognize the connection between gender and all curriculum topics and integrate it throughout the year.** "Today we're continuing our exploration of space and the solar system. I brought in some pictures of astronauts and scientists who study space. This is Mae Jemison."

- **Use persona dolls and/or puppets to introduce TGE identities and expressions into your classroom.** Persona dolls are dolls introduced by the teacher as members of the class or as visitors to the program who are treated as if they were real children with unique personalities, identities, and backgrounds. Julie Olsen Edwards, co-author of *Anti-Bias Education* (with Derman-Sparks, 2010) and a long-time persona doll user and trainer, explains:

> "Conversations with persona dolls build vocabulary and understanding for children, especially in those areas where feelings run high. The dolls' experiences unfold throughout the school year. The children quickly empathize with the dolls, who become like members of the classroom. When the children help the persona dolls deal with issues of identity, diversity, discriminatory teasing, and exclusion, they develop language to think about these issues in a climate of safety and to apply the ideas to their own lives and the life of the classroom."

Julie introduces us to one of the dolls she has used over the years to prompt conversations about gender:

Casey is a soft-body, snugly doll with curly black hair that wears a pink tutu and a bright yellow firefighter jacket, hat, and boots. When I first introduce Casey to the children they inevitably ask: "Is Casey a boy or a girl?" I respond, "What do you think?" The children have lots of ideas, and argue about who is right. Then I ask, "How could you find out?" The children are clear, "You have to ask!" So I ask by whispering in Casey's ear, put Casey to my ear to "hear" an answer, and say, "Casey doesn't want to say. Now what? How are we going to make Casey welcome?" Now the conversation turns to what Casey does and doesn't like to play. The children seem quite content that Casey's gender is no longer an issue, although the issue will continue to come up throughout the semester. –Julie Olsen Edwards

To read more about how to incorporate persona dolls into your program, read Julie's three-page handout "Working With Persona Dolls" on our website (www.genderjusticeinearlychildhood.com).

You can also use storytelling and children's literature to emphasize gender diversity. See Chapter 4 for an expanded discussion of gender inclusive literature for early childhood programs.

- **Give children opportunities to explore and express themselves using open-ended creative projects and "loose parts"** (Daly & Beloglovsky, 2018). Open-ended materials and loose parts are materials that can be moved, carried, combined, redesigned, lined up, and taken apart and put back together in multiple ways (Daly & Beloglovsky, 2014). They are materials with no specific set of directions that can be used alone or combined with other materials. Examples include: stones, stumps, sand, gravel, fabric, twigs, wood, pallets, balls, buckets, baskets, crates, boxes, logs, rope, tires, shells, and seedpods (Daly & Beloglovsky, 2014; Nicholson, 1971). Open-ended materials support children's development of agency and self-expression because children are able to use the materials to create their own constructions and to tell their own stories, including narratives about gender. Open-ended materials and loose parts support children to communicate the ideas and feelings they have about gender—not only their own gender but also how they are making sense of gender in the world around them. When children use loose parts in many different ways on a daily basis, they have opportunities to reflect their daily experiences in their families and communities while also imagining and trying out new possibilities for themselves, their identities, and their lives. Loose parts are dynamic, just like identity and culture, and children can continually return to the same materials to explore and create in new ways including "trying out" new identities that they may not be supported to explore outside of the context of play. Children can use loose parts and open-ended materials to play out narratives where they have power and agency to identify with the gender that is most authentic to them—inverting the reality of their daily experiences.

- **Reflect gender diversity in posters, art, and decorations.** Scan your classroom and notice the posters, art, and decorations you have adorning your walls. Who is represented? What genders do you see? Are all of the bodies implicitly communicating (or explicitly labeled) only "girl" and "boy"? Or do you have images representing of bodies and gender expressions around the classroom? Support children and families to see gender diversity reflected all around the classroom through images, art, and decorations. You might hang pictures of people with diverse bodies and diverse gender presentations engaged in various activities in the dress-up area in your classrooms. For example, male-presenting ballet dancers, female-presenting construction workers, drag queens, nonbinary-presenting doctors, and others. As children look around their classroom, these images reinforce messages of your value for and acknowledgment of gender diversity as a natural aspect of children, families, and humanity.

• Some programs such as those inspired by the educational philosophy of Reggio Emilia don't put posters and decorations on their walls, but do hang photos and artwork from the classroom and other documentation of the children's thinking and exploring. If you work in a program like this, be intentional about documenting a range of gender exploration in play and thought.

Use language that supports gender diversity. Whether or not we think we're talking about gender, we're talking about gender, because binary gender runs throughout our language. The language that we use in our everyday lives is the primary way that we make sense of and understand the world around us. The more deeply we ingrain a binary sense of gender into our language, the more strongly we are likely to believe in only binary possibilities of gender in ourselves and others. In the English language, we divide ourselves along binary gender lines in subconscious and mundane ways all the time. We address our students with "Good morning, boys and girls!" We convey respect with "sir" or "madam" (or "miss"). Following are some ways you can begin to use language that supports gender diversity:

• **Address the children in gender inclusive ways.** Instead of saying "boys and girls," try: "Good morning!" "Let's gather over here, friends." "Happy Friday, everyone!" Use inclusive or specific terms to refer to groups of children, instead of referring to groups of children by gender. Examples of inclusive terms include: "children," "kids," "friends," "everyone." Here are some examples of specific terms one could use in a situation where several children are riding bicycles recklessly—instead of "Boys, slow down" say "Jun-Ho and Lewis, slow down!" (use names), or "Bikers, slow down!" or "Superheroes, slow down!"

- **During transitions, dismiss, call on, and group children in a variety of ways rather than by gender.** To get them into partners or small groups, try something like "Turn to your elbow partner" or "Get in three groups—glitter, sparkle, and sequins." Instead of saying "Girls, line up to head outside," try something like "Everyone with green on their clothes may head outside."

- **When talking about animals, plants, or objects, use gender-neutral pronouns or a variety of pronouns,** rather than always using "he" as a default. You might say, "The snail is extending its tentacles! You're holding them very calmly."

Gender binary language is everywhere: we have to notice this before we can begin to use language that supports gender diversity

Every time we—teachers, parents, and students—use a pronoun, we are making a statement about gender: usually a "This is what gender I'm guessing that person is"-type of statement, and most often without verbal confirmation that this pronoun is correct. I'm guilty of it too...however many times I tell the children, "You can't tell someone's gender just by looking at them," me, their parents, other teachers, and everyone they meet everywhere are demonstrating just the opposite. —Encian, Preschool Teacher

As you become more and more aware of the gendered language that you use every day, you may start to see ways that those words are limiting and prescriptive, rather than open-ended and descriptive of all the variety there is around you. Addressing a group of children as "boys and girls" forces those children to categorize themselves as one or the other, while some children may feel they belong in both groups or may like to travel between the two. Other children might not be comfortable with either label. Even children who fit comfortably in one or the other can be limited by gendered language. Many gendered words come with associations and expectations that might make any child (or adult) feel constricted and uncomfortable.

Because words are so powerful, we want to make sure that we become more and more conscious of how and when we use gendered language. To do that **we recommend first picking a day on which you will try not to use any gendered words at all.** For the whole day. We haven't made it yet, so don't despair if you don't get past breakfast! Keep a journal with you, and take notes throughout the day.

- How many times did you slip up?

- What were the words that got past you?

- Did it get easier as the day went on?

- Just how mentally exhausting was it to do?

- How many words did you have to rethink and replace?

- What were some of them?

- How many times do you think you used a word and didn't even catch yourself?

Once you have an idea of just how much gender creeps into your day-to-day language, you can start to find alternatives where appropriate. At this point, we encourage you not to despair that it's too much to change, or to jump to the extreme of trying to eliminate all gendered language completely. **Just take manageable steps towards using language deliberately and in ways that are open-ended and descriptive.**

> *I've been given these new frameworks and they're hard to get in my head. They're confusing. They're new. It's a struggle. I have all these intentions of having this more flexible thinking around gender and sharing that with children, and I also still reinforce binaries and I still do things that cause harm... It takes practice and there's no shame in that. –Kate, Early Childhood Equity Trainer*

In your journal, look through some of the language you jotted down. Are there phrases you use that reinforce binary gender and might leave some children out? Can you think of words that might be more open-ended and inclusive? Are there words you use that have associations and expectations that are prescriptive and limit a child's gender agency instead of being descriptive? For example, "Oo, you look like a princess!"

would be a prescriptive statement, while, "Oo, you're wearing the green lace dress with the sparkly purple crown!" would be descriptive. Can you work on using those gendered words only when they fit the child you're describing? This doesn't mean eliminating gendered words altogether, but rather being conscious and intentional in your use of gendered language. Splitting a group into "princes and princesses" may very well alienate some children, but that doesn't mean you can't still make that one child's eyes light up by saying they look like a magical prince or princess!

Here are some manageable steps to help you move towards language that feels comfortable and affirming for you and the children you work with:

- In a journal, begin to make note of the types of gendered words and phrases you use most.

- Ask yourself if that language is open-ended and descriptive, allowing children freedom to identify, express, and explore their genders confidently.

- Start implementing new language, a little at a time. Explore words for yourself and with children that feel validating and empowering.

- Try not to use gendered language in reference to others without first asking what kinds of words they use for themselves. This means:

  - working hard not to ascribe a gender to strangers, and teaching children to do the same.

  - normalizing the practice of asking about and sharing pronouns as early as possible. Let children know that they can decide how they want others to talk to and about them, and they can change their mind if they feel differently later.

Below we describe some examples of common gendered language in early childhood spaces and some possible alternatives that are more open-ended and descriptive. Remember, though, that the words you use with children should be words that work for you in your environment. Ask your children what kinds of words they want to use to describe themselves and each other. Make sure that everyone feels good about the language in your learning space.

Common gendered language in early childhood and more gender inclusive alternatives[1] (Smith & Pastel, 2018)

Instead of...	Try...
"Boys and girls", "ladies and gentlemen", "You guys"	Children, students, kids, comrades, everyone, everybody, folks, you all, team
"Look at that woman over there. She has a cool hat."	"Look at that person over there. They have a cool hat." [Not assigning gender to strangers.]
"He's a hungry little caterpillar!"	"It's a hungry little caterpillar!" [Or "she," or "they"; resist defaulting to male gender on every animal and inanimate object you encounter.]
"Boys have penises, girls have vaginas."	"Many boys have penises, some don't. Many girls have vaginas and vulvas, some don't." "Some people with penises are not boys. Some people with vaginas are not girls."
"You were born a girl." "He was born a girl."	"When you were born we guessed you were a girl. You get to decide if that is true." "He has a body that made grown-ups guess he was a girl when he was born, but he's the only one who can say who he is." [Body parts ≠ gender.]
"You're a boy because you have a penis."	"You get to decide if you're a boy, girl, both, or someone else." [Child has agency.]
Always giving compliments that reinforce stereotypes—e.g., telling boys they're strong, good builders, and praising their actions, while we tell girls they're pretty, have nice clothes, and are kind.	Purposely switch gendered comments. For example, tell boys how pretty or kind they are; tell girls how strong or tough they are.
When children ask, "Is that a boy or a girl?"	"I don't know. If they were a friend of ours, we could ask." [Not assigning gender to strangers.]
What other gendered language have you found that you use?	Add to this list additional examples of more open-ended and descriptive language you can use with young children!

---

1   Note: we recommend adapting this list to use words and phrasing that fits your own authentic vocabulary and speech patterns.

Exploring gender through roles in imaginary play
Creating the opportunity for children to have "a gender sandbox"

> *Pretend…is the stage upon which any identity is possible, and secret thoughts can be safely revealed. (Paley, 1990, p. 7)*

As previously discussed, gender identity is a social identity. Gender is learned through our use of language ("she," "he," "them,") and cultural and organizational routines (e.g., how chores and responsibilities are assigned in families, how restrooms are designed in buildings, how clothing is marketed and sold in stores) as well as adult modeling of the social norms and expectations in families and communities (how to greet others, how to express emotions and handle conflict, etc.). Gender is continually experienced through relationships with other people. For a young child, the most important relationships are with the caregivers and individuals who are most familiar and consistent: family, peers, and others who are present to the child (such as bus drivers, doctors, staff members from a place of worship, among others). When gender is a topic that creates conflict and tension in a child's most familiar and consistent relationships, their developing identity and sense of self can be under assault on a daily basis—an experience likely to negatively impact their learning and development.

Having the opportunity to try on another gender expression or identity in the context of play can ease this tension for the child. The play context becomes a kind of "sandbox" for gender exploration without the weight of family or cultural expectations. Of course, the sandbox can also become a conflict- and tension-filled space when children's gender exploration is resisted by other children. **It is our job as teachers to protect the space of the sandbox as a "yes and" space of expansive play and inclusion,** and help children resolve conflicts so that it does not turn into a trauma-inducing environment of "You can't!" (A *"you can't"* logic dictates: "You can't wear a dress, you are a boy!", "You can't be Spiderman, you are a girl!". A *"you can"* logic allows "You can wear a dress *and* be a boy!", "You can be Spiderman and be a girl!")

Play is the most important and natural context for young children to explore and to learn about who they are in the world. Free play may be the only opportunity children have to explore gender creatively and free from the control of other adults and children throughout their daily interactions. Taking on roles in play and playacting across different gender identities and expressions can be especially liberating for current or future TGE children. Why is this the case? Let's consider some of the important experiences children can have when they play:

- **Children can "try on" different genders in fantasy play.** Children of all genders enjoy trying on different roles in play. Any teacher of young children will have seen their fair share of cats, dogs, lions, horses, princesses, superheroes, babies, and other pretend roles in the classroom. Children use play to explore and expand different identities and aspects of themselves and to organize their understanding of the world around them. We opened this chapter with an anecdote about a child, Lucien, who played a "Sisters" game with a friend so often that the children and Lucien themself began to think of and refer to Lucien as a girl. What can it look like to support young children to try on different genders in the context of play? Here is a window into what this looks like for one preschool:

Two other children who were designated male at birth have been playing a similar "Sisters" game. Keldan, four, describes themself as "an in-betweener pretending to be a boy" and often plays "Sisters" with a group of girls in their class. They make a home in the play structure, surviving in the forest without parents. Jacob, five, describes himself as a boy and occasionally wears skirts or dresses to school. The other children and adults are used to seeing him in a skirt, and don't make a big deal out of it. Jacob's best friend, Ryan, also a boy, likes wearing dresses sometimes too. One day, Teacher Michael is facilitating an art project. Jacob crawls onto a chair and looks at the materials on the table. "Sister!" he says in his baby voice, "Come look at this!" The two sisters (Ryan and Keldan) come to the table to check out the project. Nobody reacts as exploration with gender identity and expression is integrated naturally into this classroom. Later in the year, Jacob plays "Brother and sister." Annette is the brother, and Jacob is the sister. They live by themselves with no parents and play a lot of basketball. Jacob enjoys the game so much, he tells his mom all about it when he goes home.

Fantasy play allows children to safely explore gender roles that are off-limits in their daily lived experiences. This can include amplified cisgender roles! For example, in some coded female roles—princess, queen, ballerina—gender is exaggerated, giving children of all genders who play these roles a chance to assume aspects of feminine expression (typically fanciness and prettiness, although increasingly also power, as Disney and popular culture updates its princess archetype) that they may not get to inhabit in their day-to-day experiences. Similarly, in coded male roles like warrior and specific male superheroes, children of all genders who play these roles have a chance to assume aspects of masculine expression (typically aggression and control) that might not be available to them in daily life.

- **Playing non-human animals and other gender-neutral characters, like robots, monsters, and even babies, allows children to explore identities outside of binary gender options.** While some children specify a gender when adopting these roles—as in, the boy wolf and the girl cheetah—these clarifications are only necessary for roles that do not in themselves display typically gendered behavior. Although media representations of non-human animals do their best to overlay human gender roles onto them (adding long eyelashes and lipstick to many a female beast) any child who observes a pet or wildlife can understand that this is unnecessary and not a direct reflection of the natural world. Similarly, children can pretend to be babies and role-play a wide range of behaviors—spitting up, crying, smiling, nursing, discovering their fingers, being rocked to sleep, and more—without needing a designated gender role.

- **Through play, children can liberate themselves from overwhelming feelings, worries, and concerns.** It is common for children to use play to act out their worries and concerns instead of talking about them. Children use toys, materials, and pretend play to express what they cannot verbalize ("I don't like being called a girl"), do things they would otherwise feel uncomfortable doing (trying out a different gender), and express feelings they might be reprimanded for verbalizing (showing anger, sadness, or power over an adult who won't let them use their chosen name and pronoun). Play gives children a way to express aspects of their inner world that may be too frightening to express directly.

By acting out a situation in pretend play, children can release and express their true feelings, with less fear of the punishment or judgment they too often experience when they try to share the same information outside of a play context. Additionally, when children return to an interaction, experience, or event over and over and change or reverse the outcome in play in a manner that acknowledges their wishes and desires (e.g., pretending that they are allowed to change their pronoun or that they can make certain body parts appear or disappear), they are more able to cope with, or adjust to, the problem as it exists in real life. In this way, play supports children to express themselves authentically, which can help them manage their overwhelming feelings.

- Paulie, an adult transgender person, shares an early play memory:

I had no language or understanding that I could be a boy in real life, but in fantasy play I was always being a boy! One of my earliest memories is playing with my little sister and saying, 'I'm a boy, and I'm seven.' It sounded very old, so I must have been four or five at the time. I pretended to make sandwiches for the family. Fantasy play was so important for me, it was how I expanded and created myself when I was otherwise a very shy, insular kid. If I wasn't playing out stories with other kids, I would play them out privately in my head. It's still important today—it's still how I invent myself! I think we don't hear that enough: play never stops being necessary.

Story writing and acting

Teachers can also support children's imaginary play by introducing story writing and acting into the curriculum (Paley, 2004). Story writing supports children to imagine themselves as protagonists in stories they create. Children then share their stories with their peers, and the children take different roles and act out each narrative. When children's stories are shared with the group, everyone gets a chance to see and hear each other's ideas, to make sense of the world around them, and to imagine who they are and who they can become. Below is an example of how story writing and story acting supports children's gender exploration in one early childhood program:

In our three-year-olds classroom, children have been creating open-ended art (paintings, collage, sculpture, buildings, etc.), and dictating and acting out stories based on the art over the course of the year. Throughout the year, Idara (a presumed boy) kept creating versions of the same story, involving a boy, a mom, and a tiger. Sometimes the tiger would eat the boy, and sometimes the mom would shoot the tiger. Idara would switch which character he played—he started off playing the boy, but soon switched to playing the mom. Then for a while, instead of a boy and mom he wrote a girl and mom, and Idara wanted to be the girl several times in a row. Then for the rest of the year he was always the tiger, and the tiger ate everyone. He began playing animals more and more often in fantasy play, as well—sometimes explaining that he was a "girl" tiger, sometimes a "boy" tiger. He never expressed interest in being a girl outside of play that I could pick up on. But the play and the playacting allowed him to experience these different roles and expand his range of self.

Remember, when a child pretends to be a gender other than their assumed or legally designated gender, this does not indicate that they are transgender or destined to become transgender. This message bears repeating. Just as a boy who wishes to wear a dress is often *not* expressing a need to transition to a female identity, but simply *likes* dresses, so too is it the case that a girl who wishes to play a brother is often *not* expressing a need to transition to a male identity, but simply wishes to *pretend to be a brother,* temporarily.

Taking play seriously

In addition to making sure that there is ample time for free play in your daily schedule, teachers can support children to play, create, and express themselves in ways that invite, acknowledge, and value gender diversity by adopting and integrating the following practices:

- **Take children's play seriously and observe how children are exploring gender in their play.** Notice a child's tendency to choose specific roles and gender pronouns in their imaginative play. For infants and toddlers: Though they may not use pronouns, notice patterns in terms of materials, tools, colors, and spaces the children gravitate to. Ask yourself: Are these items gendered? Am I gendering them for the children? Do the child's preferred play materials and practices inform how I am perceiving their developing gender identity and gender expression? Remain aware of subtle messages you are communicating about which fantasy roles and types of play are appropriate or inappropriate for children of different genders. Actively work to encourage all types of roles and play (e.g., take apart gendered costumes and mix the different parts into one big costume bin).

- **Track locations in the classroom where children prefer to play and areas they avoid. Help them expand their range of play into different parts of the classroom.** Notice where children naturally gravitate, and support their engagement, while also introducing them to other objects and activities. For example, for a child who always plays with trucks in the sand area, introduce other objects (e.g., dolls, kitchen tools) to that space. "Jay hasn't visited the art center once this year. He's very interested in superheroes… I wonder what would happen if I put some blank masks out with the art supplies?" Intervene when certain play areas become known for gendered types of play. The block area can be a high-action area, and often the quieter children are pushed out. A teacher might say, "I see so many of you playing with the blocks with great active energy! Moshe wants to play in this space with quieter energy. What other ways can we play with the blocks to include them?"

- **Notice when children are segregating by gender or limiting themselves to certain types of play based on stereotypical gender norms, and make a plan to intervene.** "Hmm, looks like Janine, Adeline, and Yemaya are playing that princess game in the dress-up corner again. Their script hasn't changed, and they keep fighting over that one dress. I want to think of a way to expand their play narrative." When you notice that children are limiting themselves based on gender norms, help them expand their type of play, play narratives, and playmates. You can rotate what you have available in the dress-up area, put out books that expand their play scripts (e.g., princesses who have adventures and rescue people and do more than just look pretty and marry princes), and then invite the children to act out one of the stories together at circle time. When children's storylines seem "stuck," teachers can also enter children's play and ask questions that guide children to think of new dimensions that expand their roles ("What do the princesses do on the weekend? Who are the other people in the princesses' families? What do they like to do with their friends and family? Where do they go to school? What do they want to learn?"). When children are segregating themselves into opposing groups based on gender, you can encourage gender integration by placing children who don't often play together into partners or small groups for activities, or during play or transitions such as going on walks. Be mindful of whether you are reinscribing binary gender with obviously boy–girl pairings.

- **Allow more flexible use of toys and materials in different areas of the classroom.** Too often in early childhood classrooms, blocks, trains, and cars are materials that are primarily used by boys, whereas dolls and dramatic play materials are more often used by girls. Teachers can work to disrupt these patterns by allowing children to move toys and materials around the classroom. When teachers allow dolls, stuffed animals, play food, dress up, and figurines to be integrated into building and vehicle play areas or the reverse, teachers open up new possibilities for children to expand their play beyond traditionally male or female coded areas and toys in the classroom.

- **Expand the dress-up clothing available for children's play.** In a marvelously short and practical article on creating trans-friendly preschool classrooms, Laurel Dykstra (2005) suggests putting your dress up in a box that you can move around your classroom—"near the trucks one week and by the paints another time" (Dykstra, 2005, p.11). If your dress-up collection includes items traditionally coded female and male (dresses, ties, suit jackets, construction helmets, sparkly shoes, etc.), it is important that these items are balanced with each other. That is, you don't want to have all dresses and sparkly shoes, but instead to have a balance of items traditionally coded male and female available for children. It is also really important to include a number of gender-neutral items (sparkly tunics, animal suits or accessories, jumpsuits, etc.). Dress-up clothing should come in an array of sizes. Another strategy that many teachers use is to replace costumes with open-ended dress-up items, such as fabric pieces or scarves.

Responding to gender bias in children's play

So far we've approached gender exploration and diversity in curriculum, and talked about applying a gender justice lens to everything from the language you use to the materials you set out. In a liberated world where bias has been eradicated, supporting diversity and personal agency might be enough—and we can work towards this world. However, research shows that children use play to reproduce all of the inequalities they see in the world around them (Grieshaber & McArdle, 2010). Therefore, **we must help children learn to recognize gender bias, and advocate for themselves and others in the face of bias and injustice.**

We provided you with some practical strategies for reducing your own gender bias, and in Chapter 6, we discuss responding to the bias of other adults in the classroom. Now, let's look at how to respond to bias that occurs among children in our programs. Some common ways gender bias shows up include misgendering and eliminating or limiting other people's agency, repeating harmful stereotypes, teasing, and exclusion. **How can you respond when gender bias shows up with the children in your care?** Let's explore some promising approaches to addressing gender bias:

- **Acknowledge that children absorb the gender norms and expectations from the world around them, and many will "police" their peers and actively work to reinforce the gender binary.** An important beginning step for early childhood teachers is to acknowledge that children can and do reproduce the inequities all around them in their beliefs and behaviors even at very young ages. Traditional child development theory described children as innocent and egocentric, which led to false assumptions—still widely accepted today—that children are not aware of power differences and inequities in society (racism, classism, sexism, etc.) or capable of participating in marginalizing others. Research has discredited the belief that children are immune from the forces of oppression and prejudice, and we have many studies and books that document how children reproduce harmful behaviors they see modeled for them by adults in their families, communities and media.

Acknowledging this fact is a start for early childhood teachers. Only when we open our eyes to observing these behaviors can they be disrupted through our own intervention and, ideally, in collaboration with children who can learn to "see" inequity and advocate for themselves and others to be treated fairly and respectfully.

- Kelly, a former preschool teacher in a corporate center, describes a culture of gender bias in the classroom:

  The girls that spoke up and were loud and wanted to take control, they were ridiculed by the boys. It was like, "Well, she's running around and trying to tell us what to do," and it was like she was acting out of her girl box. Then on the opposite side, there were young boys who wanted to play in a corner and had soft voices, and loved to draw, and didn't want to run, and didn't want to play on the playground, and just wanted to sit at the table and work with Teacher Kelly, and just draw, and be very quiet, and wear something different, wear a little hat, like a little fedora. Those little boys stuck out in a different way, and often, had some of the same issues with boys in the group as well so they would get bullied. So when the boys were acting out of the boy box, they were ridiculed as well.

- **Do not shame or get upset with children. Teach them.** As teachers, we never want to shame children or do further harm. Our first responsibility is to the person(s) who are harmed: to provide support, safety, and protection. Our next responsibility is to the person whose words or behavior led to the harm: our approach should be one of teaching and not punishing or shaming them. We want to guide children to learn about how their words or behavior impacts their peers and others—both positively and negatively—and to focus continuously on the shared agreements and values of the classroom community (e.g., treat one another with respect, care for yourself and others, make good choices). When we observe children using language or behaving in ways that discriminate, tease, exclude, or otherwise harm others, teachers have a range of options available for educating children as these are your most critical teachable moments. It is important to intervene when children display gender bias by their limiting or enforcing each other's gender expression or identities in play, making negative comments about a person's appearance or capabilities, excluding on the basis of gender, or using stereotypes to inform beliefs. Below are several strategies early childhood teachers can use to effectively respond to challenging interactions in the classroom where children's words and behaviors reflect the biases they are learning from the world they are living in.

In the moment

Intervene in moments of gender bias between children by asking open-ended questions and gathering information without blaming or shaming children. Practice this throughout all the types of bias situations including those listed below. Pause the game, for example: "Nikki, what did you mean when you said this is a girl game?" (See the box "Teacher intervention in gender biasis" near the end of this chapter for an example of a teacher using inquiry to address bias.)

Always intervene when children...

- Make stereotypical or prejudicial remarks about gender. Name and discuss the stereotypes, and how they are unfair and can hurt people. (Remember, a stereotype is a generalization about a group of people that isn't true of everyone in that group.) Offer clear, accurate information that contradicts children's stereotypes and false ideas about gender. Practice using words like "most" or "many" instead of "all". Teacher: "It's true that many of the girls in our class have long hair. But so do some of the boys and in-betweeners!"

- Misgender each other or resist each other's gender agency: "Adi can't have a penis because Adi is a girl!" Teacher: "Actually, Adi gets to decide who they are, and Adi gets to name their own body parts. Just like you get to decide who you are."

- Assign each other roles based on gender. A toddler points to the infant next to her and says, "He is brother because he is boy." Or preschooler Adam says, "Miles, you have to be the dad because you're a boy." Miles replies, "But I want to be the sister!" Teacher: "How about Miles can be the sister this time? It seems really important to him. Let's see if anyone else wants to play the dad!" (asks other children, without regard to gender).

- Exclude each other from play based on gender and other social identities and/or physical attributes. See the box "Exploring Exclusion" near the end of this chapter.

- Make space for deeper discussion between all affected parties. When Teacher Heather took Lucien and Emma outside, sat with them, validated their feelings, and asked them if they had questions or things to say to each other, she created the conditions for dialogue between the two that led to greater understanding.

- Trust the children. By asking a series of open-ended questions, we help children do their own deep thinking about bias, and understand why it hurts and is unfair on a much deeper level than if we just tell them what we think. When we trust children to work out and solve their own problems, they tend to rise to the occasion, often in creative ways we couldn't anticipate.

- If an adult makes a comment about children's play that reveals heteronormative assumptions, address it in a diffusing way and check-in with the adult later. For example, a grandfather who is visiting the classroom comments, "Jeremy always talks about wanting to marry Rachelle." Teacher says, "Yah, he's thinking a lot about creating families. Yesterday, he and Steven were planning their wedding too." Or a parent states: "He started running around so fast! All that boy energy is a lot harder to keep up with than when Julia was little." Teacher responds, "Yes, there is such a range of temperaments and energy levels with infants and toddlers! Maya and Arlen are similarly high energy like your child: I sometimes have a hard time keeping up with them myself!"

Following up

- **Ask the entire class for their ideas.** When conflicts around gender or gender-based exclusion arise, ask children if you can share the story of what happened with the class and get their help working it out. Support the children to solve problems related to unfairness around gender. Reinforce that classroom rules generated together might be different than rules at home or in other places.

- **Use persona dolls or puppets** to address gender bias in the classroom without putting individual students on the spot. Teacher: "What's that, Carmen? Ah. Carmen wants me to tell you about what happened on the playground after she got her new haircut. Some kids were saying, 'You're a boy! You're a boy!' and laughing at her. How do you think that made her feel? [Takes answers from children] ... If you were there on the playground, what could you do to help?"

- **Address bias in other ways in the curriculum.**

  - Read books that address gender bias or, better yet, that show the accepting classroom culture we're trying to create (see Chapter 4).

  - Discuss "stereotypes" as a group, and practice identifying them. Practice using words like "most" and "many" rather than "all."

  - When children notice gender bias from teachers or other adults in the classroom, or in the world outside the classroom, create space to discuss what they have seen and how they feel about it. Support children in taking individual, small-group, and collective action (see the box "Collective action" near the end of this chapter.).

Teacher intervention in gender bias

Kenny walks up to a group of children involved in a fantasy-play game on the yard of a four-to-five-year-old classroom. "What are you playing?" Kenny asks Béatriz, who seems to be at the center of the game. "I'm the king," she says. "Those are my fire ninjas." Kenny cracks up, laughing, "King? You can't be a king! You have to be a queen." Teacher Maxa (they/them pronouns) overhears this exchange. They walk over to the children and wait a moment to see how Béatriz will respond. Béatriz puts her hands on her hips. "I can be a king if I want," she tells Kenny. "No you can't!" Kenny replies, continuing to laugh. There is a moment of silence. The other children are hesitant to stand up to Kenny, and wait to see how this will play out.

Teacher Maxa decides to intervene. "Kenny, why did you say Béatriz can't be the king?"

"Because she's a girl. Girls are queens, boys are kings."

"Not at our school," Maxa tells him. "Béatriz gets to decide who she is, and you get to decide who you are. Do you want to play this game too?"

"No." Kenny wanders away. He's stopped laughing. Maxa turns to Béatriz.

"Béatriz, I didn't like it when he was laughing at you. Do you want him to check-in with you?"

But Béatriz is back to commanding her fire ninjas. "No thanks," she says. Later, Maxa decides to follow up the incident with a puppet show that explores how people feel when they are laughed at.

In this situation, Teacher Maxa does not jump in immediately to respond to a "You can't!" challenge but first gives the children a chance to respond themselves. In a two- or three-year-old classroom, Maxa might jump in sooner, but the fours and fives at their school have had practice with this, and they wait until the children get stuck. Next, they ask a question to find out more about why Kenny was challenging Béatriz's play. When Kenny confirms that it is about gender roles, Maxa repeats and rephrases Béatriz's original response, reminding Kenny that each child gets to pick who they are for themself, not for others. This is a basic message that children understand, and also translates nicely from the realm of play to the realm of identity. ("I'm not a girl, I'm a boy. I decide who I am, you decide who you are.") In this case, Maxa addresses the content of the challenge—you can be a king, even if you're a girl—but they do not address the fact that by laughing, Kenny was teasing Béatriz. They could call Kenny back over and talk with him about this or ask him to check-in with Béatriz about her feelings, but in this case they decide to let the play continue and follow up later with a discussion about teasing with the entire class.

Exploring exclusion

Teachers of young children everywhere deal with exclusionary play in their classrooms and playgrounds, and they have developed many ways to deal with it. In her 1992 book *You Can't Say You Can't Play*, Vivian Paley tells the story of a year-long experiment conducted by her kindergarteners to test whether this new rule, "You can't say you can't play," will work to facilitate inclusive play (Paley, 1992). While some teachers employ this sort of blanket rule to address exclusion, others take a more situational approach. As one teacher explains, "A no-exclusion rule might work, but at the end of the day it's imposed by adults. I want our students to practice navigating these situations so that they have strategies to use when they're at their next school, or at the park, and they don't have a rule or adults to fall back on."

While there may be some circumstances for a teacher to allow exclusionary play, exclusion on the basis of social or physical differences is a form of bias, and it is never okay. We asked teachers from a range of program styles how they intervene in these moments of exclusion. Here is a summary of their answers:

Ask questions to find out more about the situation. Give all children who are involved in the situation a chance to speak.

Address bias even when bias is not the root motivating factor for exclusion. Often the reason children give for exclusion—e.g., "He can't play because he's a boy"—is just an excuse off the top of their head and not the underlying reason. If you address it—"Did you think boys can't be ponies?"—they will often switch to something else, like "Well... this is just a two-person game." Regardless of the motivation behind a statement of exclusion based on differences (like "He can't play because he's a boy"), it still has an impact—in this case, to delineate gender roles and normalize gender segregation. It has an impact on the child who is being excluded, those who are doing the excluding, and everyone nearby who witnesses the interaction. This is why it is so important to intervene in these moments and problematize this sort of bias, even when it is not the underlying reason for exclusion. The intervention can be quick ("That's actually not true" or "Tell me more about why you think that"), but it needs to be there.

Address children's underlying fears. Often the underlying reason children exclude is because they are enjoying the game they're playing, and they're worried that a new person will change the game. This is a valid concern! As teachers, we can help deflate the fear by addressing it directly, help children see the positive in what the new child could bring to the game, and help them find a role in their game for the new person. "Keldan, it seems to me that you're worried that Errol will turn this into a fighting game. Is that true? But yesterday Errol played ponies with Lilah, so I know he knows how. If you tell him this is not a fighting game, he will listen. Right, Errol?"

Counter stereotypes. Other times, the underlying reason really is connected to the cited difference. In the above example, Keldan is mixing what he knows about Errol—he likes fighting games—with what he is coming to believe about boys in general: boys only like fighting games. In this case, we teachers need to stop the stereotype as it is forming: "Boys play ninjas. They don't play ponies." Teacher: "A lot of boys in our class do like to play ninjas right now. But some girls do too. Ananke and Victoria like to play ninjas. And Béatriz. And Raul plays ponies all the time!" We may decide to address this in the curriculum in other ways, especially if it is a thought that has popped up more than once: for instance, making sure we are giving examples of boys playing ponies and other coded-female games, and of girls playing ninjas and other coded-male games through puppet shows, persona dolls, storytelling, books, and images we have around the classroom.

Help the children notice exclusion by restating what is happening. "Kenny and Raul say Ananke can't go on the structure with them. That sounds like they're excluding her. Ananke, how does that feel?"

Appeal to the excluded person's sense of fairness. "Ananke, Kenny says you can't play because you're a girl. Does that sound fair to you?" Often, more children will join the conversation about whether this is fair or not.

Restate the rules the children are making and ask if they are fair. One teacher points out that around the age of four, children are discovering rules and their ability to make them. Often what sounds like exclusion—"Only people with long hair can come in the loft"—is a way of experimenting with rule setting. Again, teachers can help children examine whether their rules are fair, and we can shine a light on how these rules impact other children. Teachers can challenge children to come up with rules for their space which include everyone who wants to play.

Collective action

Children in an outdoor summer camp noticed that the outhouse at the park their camp used was split into binary bathroom choices: male and female. "That's not fair!" one of the children exclaimed. "What about our friends who aren't girls or boys? Where can they go pee?" Teachers allowed this child to voice their concerns with the rest of the group, and soon all the children were impassioned about the issue. Teachers helped the children identify the park ranger as someone to voice their concerns to. They found the ranger and talked. The ranger was sympathetic but explained that she couldn't change the signs. The children were discouraged. Teachers helped the children channel their feelings into art; together, they painted many signs expressing their thoughts—"Bathrooms are for everyone!" and "This isn't fair!" and "We all deserve to pee"—and posted the signs all over the outhouse. Seeing their work displayed publicly and prominently, the children left camp that day feeling empowered to act together for change.

Self-study and classroom audit tool: classroom/program culture

Use the statements below as a guide to assess the level of gender justice developing in your program's culture. This area of change is typically a longer-term goal, as the small changes we incorporate into our everyday practices become second nature for teachers and children alike. These statements are intentionally written to ask you to observe how children are enacting the values of gender justice that you and your co-workers have instilled in the program, because that is one way to see that you are succeeding in creating change that the children will carry forward with them.

1. Children show comfort in exploring and trying on different gender identities and/or expressions.

2. Children demonstrate an understanding that gender doesn't have to be fixed or permanent.

3. Friendship, play, and social interaction among children of different genders is part of the classroom culture.

4. Children validate and support each other's gender expressions and identities, including using requested names and pronouns.

5. Children recognize gender bias and stereotypes in the classroom and in the world, and understand that these hurt people.

6. Children respond to gender bias in supportive, constructive ways, and seek to right wrongs.

7. Children have words for genders besides "boy" and "girl," and use them.

8. Children ask newcomers to share their gender pronouns rather than making assumptions.

Self-study and classroom audit tool: environments and materials

Use the statements below as a guide to think about the environment you create in your program, including visuals, books, and activity spaces. Thinking about the way we organize space and utilize materials can be a good early area for concrete action steps towards gender justice. It can also be an area where financial resources make a big difference. However, every program can be improved with some attention to how gender plays out in our environments and materials.

1. Bathrooms and toilets are not segregated by gender.

2. Posters, photos, and other visual material in the classroom include depictions of human children (not just cartoon animals or other non-human characters) and adults with a range of visible gender expressions, body sizes, skin tones, and visible disabilities, engaged in a range of pursuits.

3. Extra clothes bins are labeled by type of clothing rather than by gender.

4. Children's cubbies are not segregated by gender.

5. Posters showing anatomical body parts are not labeled "boy" and "girl."

6. The school library includes multiple positive books with transgender and gender expansive protagonists who reflect our qualities to look for in gender expansive children's literature.

7. Majority of books in the school library resist harmful gender role stereotypes. Books that perpetuate harmful gender stereotypes are removed, modified, or read with time to question and discuss stereotypes.

8. Areas with blocks, trains, and cars (traditionally coded male) are integrated with or adjacent to dramatic play areas (traditionally coded

female) such that materials including dolls, stuffed animals, play food, dress-up, and figurines can be integrated into building and vehicle play and vice versa.

9. Dolls and figurines that perpetuate harmful gender stereotypes are removed, modified, or expanded in a way that counteracts the stereotype.

10. If dress-up clothes collection includes items traditionally coded female and male (e.g. dresses, ties, suit jackets, construction helmets, sparkly shoes), these items are balanced with each other and with gender-neutral items (sparkly tunics, animal suits or accessories, jumpsuits, etc.), and come in an array of sizes.

11. Classroom materials include a variety of enticing open-ended "loose parts," which allow children to recreate themselves dynamically.

Self-study and classroom audit tool: transitions, routines, and language, and teacher-led activities

Use the statements below as a guide to think about curriculum in your program, understanding that curriculum is a very broad category in early childhood. This set of audit statements covers daily transitions, routines, activities/projects, and the language we use with children. There are countless other areas of your program and practice that could fall under curriculum. This list is just to get you thinking about where gender might show up.

1. I dismiss, call on, and group children in a variety of ways rather than by gender.

2. When conversations about anatomy come up between children, I offer clear, clarifying, affirming information without shutting down or shaming children's curiosity. I explain that body parts don't dictate gender.

3. I address my class in gender inclusive ways instead of saying "boys and girls."

4. I set up open-ended activities and projects that allow children to explore and create themselves through various artistic mediums.

5. When conflicts around gender or gender-based exclusion arise, I ask students if we can share the story of what happened with the class and get their help working it out. I use children's questions, curiosities, and ideas about gender to shape the curriculum and share stories that address those questions or counteract their stereotypes.

6. I use persona dolls or puppets to address gender bias in the classroom without putting individual students on the spot.

7. I intervene in moments of gender bias between children by asking questions and offering information without blaming or shaming children.

8. I support the children strategizing around solving problems of unfairness around gender. I reinforce that classroom rules we generate together might be different from rules at home or in other places.

9. I introduce children to gender resources and diverse gender narratives, expressions, and identities. I practice normalizing gender expansiveness by sharing narratives of TGE people that are not centered on struggle or othering.

10. I recognize the connection between gender and all curriculum topics and integrate them throughout the year.

11. I talk directly about stereotypes and practice using words like "most" and "many" rather than "all."

12. I explicitly name and identify dominant identities, like cisgender, rather than only talking about marginalized ones, like transgender identities, as examples of diversity.

13. I use inclusive or specific terms to refer to groups of children, instead of referring to groups of children by gender.

14. When I talk about people who I don't know the gender identity of, I use language that avoids assigning them a gender. I recognize that I don't truly know someone's identity unless they have shared it with me themselves.

15. When I talk about animals, plants, or objects, I use gender-neutral pronouns or a variety of pronouns, rather than always using "he" as a default.

Self-study and classroom audit tool: children's play

Use the statements below as a guide to identifying how gender shows up in children's play and how you, as a teacher, can observe, engage, and disrupt play as necessary to support gender justice. These prompts might help you think about how you would respond to certain situations that might occur when children are playing, so that you are not as often caught in the moment trying to figure out what to say.

1. I track where children play and avoid play, and I help them expand their range of play into different parts of the classroom.

2. I notice when children are segregating by gender or limiting themselves to certain types of play based on stereotypical gender norms.

3. When I notice that children are segregating or limiting themself based on gender norms, I help children expand their type of play, play narratives, and playmates.

4. I take children's play seriously, and I observe how children are exploring gender in their play.

5. I allot ample time for free play in the daily schedule.

6. I am are aware of subtle messages I am giving about which fantasy roles and types of play are appropriate or inappropriate for children of different genders. I work to encourage all types of roles and play for all children.

7. I intervene when children exclude others from play based on gender and other social identities, physical attributes, etc.

8. I intervene when certain play areas become known for gendered types of play.

9. I intervene when children display gender bias. Gender bias includes limiting or enforcing each other's gender expression or identities in play, making negative comments about a person's appearance or capabilities based on gender, and using gender stereotypes to inform beliefs. I follow up to address bias in other ways in the curriculum.

10. If an adult makes a comment about children's play that reveals cisnormative assumptions, I address it in a diffusing way and check-in with the adult later.

—— Chapter 5 ——

Gender Justice in Children's Literature

Why is children's literature important?

Decades of research highlights the wide range of benefits that result from using children's literature in classrooms (Kersten, Apol, & Pataray-Ching, 2007; Souto-Manning, 2013). Not only can reading children's books strengthen the feeling of community in classrooms and inspire children to love literacy; children's literature also supports children to develop socially, emotionally, intellectually, culturally, and aesthetically. Through books, children can be introduced to ideas, concepts, and dilemmas that are complex and contradictory, and which expand their perspectives, invite their imagination, and support them to develop empathy and compassion. Children's literature provides children with information, offers questions for them to ponder, and offers different ways for coping with stress and trauma and a range of strong human emotions. Further, through stories, children can learn about individuals, families, cultural practices and communities that are both familiar and very different from their own experiences. For this reason, many early childhood teachers use children's literature to support their goals to create inclusive and multicultural classrooms committed to an anti-bias approach that counteracts the discrimination associated with racism, classism, ableism, and other forms of oppression in our societies.

We need to do the same when it comes to gender. Children's literature could be very effective in building children's awareness of a more inclusive understanding of gender that acknowledges a wider and more flexible range of gender identities and expressions. Unfortunately, at this time there are not many books available that communicate the messages we want young children to hear when they are forming beliefs about gender and its relationship to their own and others' identities.

When thinking about the types of books we do want to have in our classroom libraries related to gender, it is helpful to consider Rudine Sims Bishop's description of mirrors, windows, and sliding doors.

Mirrors, windows and sliding glass doors

Rudine Sims Bishop (1990, p. 1) writes:

> Books are sometimes windows, offering views of worlds that may be real or imagined, familiar or strange. These windows are also sliding glass doors, and readers have only to walk through in imagination to become part of whatever world has been created or recreated by the author. When lighting conditions are just right, however, a window can also be a mirror. Literature transforms human experience and reflects it back to us, and in that reflection we can see our own lives and experiences as part of the larger human experience. Reading, then, becomes a means of self-affirmation, and readers often seek their mirrors in books.

She goes on to state, "For many years, nonwhite readers have too frequently found the search futile" (p. 1). All children need literary mirrors that reflect who they are and validate their existence, and all children need literary windows that validate the existence of others. But for many children—children of color and multiracial children, disabled children, children in non-nuclear family structures, neurodivergent children, immigrant children, poor children, children of size, and children in other marginalized cultural positions—too many books are only windows. These children receive the message that they are inferior, not important enough to be reflected in literature, or worse, reflected only through negative stereotypes. For others (children in dominant cultural positions including white, able-bodied children from middle- or upper-class heterosexual nuclear families) too many books are only mirrors. These children receive the message that their experience is the norm.

For TGE children, who rarely find mirrors among their own family members, finding mirrors in literature takes on an extra importance. Julie Olsen Edwards (2017) writes, "Invisibility erases identity and experience. Visibility affirms a child's reality and value."

Gender expansive children need mirrors but they also need their world to be seen by all children.

What qualities should early childhood teachers look for in gender expansive children's books?

How do you decide what makes a book into a mirror, a window, a sliding door? And what do you do about the stories and books you already have in circulation that may contain harmful stereotypes or other troubling content? There are several factors that teachers should look for when choosing children's books that communicate positive and gender inclusive messages to young children and their families. Following are several criteria to keep in mind as you review and select books for your classroom library. **We encourage you to look for books that:**

Meaningfully portray characters with different gender identities and gender expressions that expand, cross, or transcend the traditional male and female binary. Characters should be represented with all the complexity, individuality, and agency/initiative of other characters within the story. Gender expansive characters should not be added to storylines in a manner that simply reflects tokenism—i.e., adding representatives of underrepresented social groups symbolically in order to give the appearance of inclusion. They should be frequently included in books and we particularly need books where TGE people are the main characters of the story. Adding transgender and gender expansive characters in children's literature creates windows for every child to learn about gender and the messages our society wants to emphasize about what we are willing to acknowledge, respect, and value regarding our diversity. If children see illustrations and text reflected in storybooks that extend ideas about gender beyond fixed, male/female binary boxes, we will support them to expand their worldviews about the range of valid gender options that exist for individuals living in our world. The more that young children see TGE characters in children's literature, the greater likelihood they will develop empathy for these characters. And significantly, gender expansive children will see these characters as mirrors and learn that their gender identities and whom they truly know themselves to be inside is important and valued by others. Including TGE characters also allows all children to see possible futures for themselves as they imagine who they can become. Books that meaningfully portray TGE characters include *Único Como Yo/One of a Kind, Like Me*; *Julián Is a Mermaid*; and *I'm Jay, Let's Play*.

Meaningfully portray TGE characters who also have other aspects of their identity represented. For instance, characters of diverse body sizes, skin tones, and abilities. Additionally, characters who are neurodiverse and/or from diverse cultural backgrounds, ethnicities, religions, class cultures, and economic circumstances. Books should include TGE characters who are represented with as much complexity and individuality as other characters in the story. Why is this diversity so important?

We want to communicate to children the accurate information that gender is not separate or disconnected from other social identities, statuses, and cultural/historical contexts, but is deeply interwoven with them. From their earliest years, we want children to learn that gender expansive people are diverse individuals who come from diverse families, communities, and circumstances. If children's literature only reflects a certain demographic group of gender diverse individuals—like white, middle-class U.S. citizens—then gender expansiveness could be misunderstood to be a privilege that is only available to individuals who share this socioeconomic class and/or race and unavailable to others. The truth is that there are ways that various privileged positions (such as being white, wealthy, or passing as cisgender) do shield trans and gender expansive people from harm in many cases, but not always. Examples of books that meaningfully portray gender expansive characters as complex and unique individuals include *Único Como Yo/One of A Kind, Like Me* and *Marisol McDonald and the Clash Bash*.

Include plots that explore a wide range of topics and ideas (e.g., friendship, school, a lost pet, a sick parent, an adventure in the woods, saying goodnight, having a bad day, waiting for a new baby to arrive). In addition to compelling plots, teachers should be looking for books that include other attributes of high-quality children's literature, especially rich language, illustrations that children respond positively to, and representations of sliding doors that engage children's imaginations. **It is important that a book feels like a story, not a didactic lesson.** An example of a book that incorporates TGE expressions into a story without making them the center of the story is *Teddy's Favorite Toy*.

Focus on the positive attitudes, beliefs, and behaviors we want children to engage in. We want literature to provide inspiration for young children to discover the many amazing ways to be in the world. We want our children to build positive self-identity and pride in who they are and how they present themselves, so that if bullying occurs, they will have the assertiveness to stand up for themselves and others. Examples of books that portray gender expansive expressions in a positive light and without negative repercussion include *I'm Jay, Let's Play* and *Julián Is a Mermaid*.

Use a variety of pronouns or no pronouns. Children can learn about the relationship between gender identity, gender expression, and different pronoun options by seeing these connections made in children's books. There are several examples of books that model different possibilities for using pronouns (or not using them at all), and these stories can generate important opportunities for children to discuss and ask questions about pronouns, including the pronoun(s) they want to use and how they can learn about and then use the pronouns spoken by other children and adults. Opening up conversations about pronoun use through children's books can be expanded into discussion about gender attribution and the need to expand our understanding of gender beyond the male/female binary. Two books we recommend include *They She He Me: Free to Be!*, which introduces a variety of pronouns alongside beautifully illustrated individuals with diverse expressions, and *I'm Jay, Let's Play*, which does not include any pronouns throughout the book. Each book features end pages with tips on navigating conversations about pronouns and gender with children.

Choose books that break gender stereotypes. Books don't have to feature characters with TGE identities or clothing choices in order to break gender stereotypes. Stories about cisgender girls who rescue and fix things and cisgender boys who nurture and show vulnerability are breaking gender stereotypes. While these books, often considered "feminist," may or may not be grouped into the "TGE children's literature" category, they are nevertheless vitally important to keep in your collection, as gender stereotypes restrict all children including cisgender children, and everyone needs models they can connect with. What matters is not where you draw your lines between categories, but that you seek out books that display all of these different aspects of gender identities and expressions, including styles and behaviors.

What about books that contain traditional depictions of femininity like girls wearing dresses, or traditional depictions of masculinity like boys playing sports? Keep the attitude: gender is a celebration, for everyone! We don't support gender diversity by pretending that femininity and masculinity don't exist. It's okay, and recommended, to include books that celebrate femininity and masculinity as well as books that celebrate nonbinary expressions—but we must take care that these books are not reinforcing harmful gender stereotypes. Ideally every book about ballet will include depictions of non-girl dancers, and every book about sports will include depictions of non-boy players, but until that day comes, find one way in which the book challenges stereotypes. If you can't find one thing, we suggest you seriously question keeping that book in your collection. Kate Engle, a gender equity trainer, talks about selecting books that interrupt automatic associations we develop, such as "prettiness" with "whiteness." Her go-to books for catching the attention of children who love all things princessy and pink are *My Colors, My World* by Maya Gonzalez and *Chavela and the Magic Bubble* by Monica Brown and *Princess Hair* by Sharee Miller, books that associate these descriptors with a diversity of skin tones and bodies.

> So if there are books that are all pink, it's gonna be about girls of color. Nothing that just slots into that same very easy cultural slot in our brain that TV shows do. So if I bring it in, I'm gonna complicate it and I'm gonna expand it to be more of what I think the beauty of femininity is. –Kate

What should teachers AVOID when selecting and reading children's books about gender with young children?

We recommend that teachers look out for two main themes in books with TGE characters, topics that are often represented together:

- books that focus on negativity, and

- books that use a "gender-transgression-as-problem" plot.

Teachers should AVOID books that focus on negativity. To date, the plots of most children's books with TGE characters involve some amount of gender bias or other form of negativity. Negativity is reflected in storylines that emphasize that TGE people experience:

- bullies, heckling, and microaggressions from their peers
- a lack of support or understanding from family members
- sadness, depression, self-hate, and harm.

Typically, books that focus on negativity are very well-intentioned. Some are written by supportive family members of TGE people. The intended message of these books is often, "Be yourself. Wear what you want!" However, the unintended message that is communicated and likely being absorbed by young children is, "When you transgress gender norms (the gender binary), you will be opening yourself up to shame and ridicule and you will be marked as 'other.'" Let's consider what "negativity" looks like when we are talking about TGE children's books.

A typical plot in this genre goes something like this: A child transgresses gender norms. This is most commonly imagined and written as a boy who wears a dress, skirt, or other feminine-coded accessory. The child receives negative feedback from parents, older siblings, peers, or other community members. This negative feedback forms the main conflict of the plot. Someone supports the child in their choices, and the child ultimately develops resilience and confidence. You might be asking yourself, what is the problem with this plot? After all, the child is supported through the hardship and even overcomes it. Isn't that empowering?

Remember, "What you pay attention to grows" (Brown, 2017, p.41). Most early childhood teachers are familiar with this concept. We know that when we tell children "Don't run in the street," they hear, "Run in the street!" And so we say instead, "Stay on the sidewalk!"

The same concept applies to stories. Even if a book has a happy ending, when the bulk of the book is focused on the negative consequences of being gender expansive, it is the negative cultural responses that children will hear and remember the most. The messaging of these books is clear: if you choose to authentically express your gender identity, the response from others will be negative, even if you eventually find acceptance. The result of this kind of messaging in many cases is to discourage the child from their gender exploration or cause them to retreat into shame and hiding.

Teachers should AVOID books in which the child's gender difference forms the main problem or focus of the plot. This problem can be subtle—if we want to teach gender diversity, what better than a book that is all about that theme? The problem is that when the books about gender-normative children are about friendship and journeys and dinosaurs and pets and family and bad days and birthdays and all the possible worlds and things that these books narrate, whereas the books about TGE children are only about the experience of being gender expansive, then we are sending a strong message to all the children in the classroom about what is "normal" (valued) and what is "other" (risky, marginalized). We are teaching them that there is a norm, and a variation. This reduces TGE children to that experience of difference and otherness. We want children to view gender identities and expressions as natural extensions of our human diversity, not as an "issue." Therefore, we need stories that show children and adults just being in all their many gendered selves, and having adventures, and loose teeth, and bad days, and all the myriad things that cisgender characters get to have. Such stories will communicate to children that they are encouraged and empowered to move how they feel, dress how they feel, express their gender as they feel, and not internalize harmful gender messages that may lead them to experience shame and feel pressure to hide their authentic self from others.

"Teacher Reading Aloud to Students": Reading positive, diverse stories featuring TGE characters' resilience, joy, and self-awareness helps children to see and value TGE people and develop self-pride, empathy, and compassion for others. Credit line: Jonathan Julian.

So what should I do when I find these troubling qualities in a children's book? Even if a book has these problems, it doesn't mean you should automatically remove it from your collection. There can be some good reasons to keep the book and use it in very intentional ways to spark discussion with children. There is a strong argument for directly addressing and exploring bias in children's literature—because bias exists in the world! (And in elementary school in particular.) We do need to talk specifically about gender bias as it occurs, and stories can be a doorway into group conversations. However, when all of our books on TGE identities and expressions are about bias, it reduces those identities to the experience of bias. Here are some things to keep in mind as you review your collection:

- Ask yourself, what have the children in my classroom experienced? If gender-based bullying is an ongoing issue in your classroom, a book can be a great entryway into discussing the issues without putting certain children on the spot. (So can using a persona doll!) If however no one has yet thought to give anyone else a hard time for what they are wearing, etc., there is no need to introduce this form of teasing to your students. Build their anti-bias skills in other ways, around unfair things that are actually, concretely happening, so that the skills are there for them to call on when needed.

- Consider balance over your entire collection. Olivia Higgins of Queerly Elementary suggests an "80/20" rule of thumb—"In books as well as in teacher-led conversations, at least 80% of the content should be positive, and no more than 20% should be negative." This rule applies to your collection as well as individual books and stories. So, out of all the books in your collection that contain TGE characters, 20% can deal directly with bias these characters face or other problems, such as internalized shame and depression, as the teddy experiences in *Introducing Teddy*. The other 80% should be positive, where the characters' gender expansiveness is embraced or not even viewed as an issue. (This is a good rule to apply to other forms of bias and aspects of diversity as well!)

- Within those 20% of books that do address bias and contain some negativity, there should still be 80% positive content.

Even if you read four positive books first, one negative one can make all the difference and shut a child down. Consider the intensity as well as the frequency of the negativity depicted in the story. A character saying, "Boys can't wear dresses!" while hitting a child on the playground is much more likely to (re)traumatize listeners than a character saying, "Why are you wearing that? My dad says dresses are for girls."

Action steps teachers can take

There are many changes you can make that will have a positive impact on children and support their healthy gender development. Following are a few ways you can get started right away to use children's literature to strengthen gender justice in your classroom:

- Review your current book collection using the criteria listed above and modify your recommended reading lists accordingly.

- Be creative when reading problematic books, not only the ones in gender expansive literature but also any book in the traditional canon of children's literature including fairy tales and award winners. Change and omit pronouns, change names, and revise gendered language. What happens to Goldilocks and the Three Bears if you use male pronouns for Goldilocks or make Mama Bear the biggest? Or make two Papa Bears? Change the gender of the trucks in *Goodnight, Goodnight, Construction Site* so that they are not all male. Then go a step further, and change up pronouns for Elephant (from *Elephant and Piggie*) so that they use "he" one day and "she" another. Picture books are a great place to practice your use of the singular "they"!

- When you are reading books to children, actively notice and question stereotypes you encounter. For example, "I wonder why they drew long eyelashes on the girl mice but not the boy mice? Do girls have longer eyelashes? Let's look at our eyelashes..." Or "Hmm, that's funny—all of Alexander's friends are eating lunches that their moms packed! I wonder why only moms packed those lunches. What do you think?" (If children don't offer evidence that contradicts the stereotype, make sure you do.)

- When reading books that involve gender bias (or any kind of bias), pause throughout the story to ask questions. In this way, we can offer children valuable opportunities to practice strategies for responding to stressful or challenging experiences, and learn to think critically about issues of social justice in their daily lives. Following are examples of the types of questions we can ask children to encourage them to reflect upon and discuss gender with their peers:

  - How do you think he felt when he heard that?

  - Is that true? Is that fair?

  - If you were X what could you say? How about if you were Y? Or Z?

  - Do you think it's okay to do that? Why or why not? What could you do instead?

  - If you saw that happen in our class, how could you be a helper? How could we make it better?

  - How can we show someone that we like them just the way they are?

- Uplift excellent books! Read them. Recommend them. Write reviews of them. Place them on display shelves. Invite the authors to come talk.

- Write new books! Tell new stories!

Oral storytelling

In this chapter we focus on children's literature, because most early childhood teachers are already reading books to children. However, nearly everything in this chapter also applies to oral storytelling, where someone tells a story without reading from a book. This has been shown to engage children at an even deeper level than reading out loud (Agosto, 2016; Haven, 2007; Phillips, 2000; Sturm, 1999). Oral storytelling with preschoolers has been shown to build community among students and teachers, and support memory recall, literacy, and creative thinking. One of the great things about storytelling is that you aren't limited to the stereotypical content found in many books—you are only limited by your own imagination! If you're curious about oral storytelling but not sure where to start, try adapting a story you already know well, such as a fairy tale, or a story from your own childhood. You can find many helpful books and web videos that share tips for storytelling with various age groups, as well as tried-and-true tales. Margaret Read MacDonald's (1993) *Storyteller's Start-Up Book* is a good place to start, but watch out for traditional gender roles in the folktales she reprints. If you're in a kindergarten or elementary school classroom, try her later book (co-authored with Jennifer MacDonald Whitman and Nathaniel Forrest Whitman), *Teaching with Story: Classroom Connections to Storytelling* (2013).

Remember to apply your critical lens to these stories as well and adapt them for your own audience. We are still waiting for someone to write a gender expansive storyteller's guide—maybe it will be you!

In closing this chapter, we would like to leave you with a story that reflects how children can learn to critique gender stereotypes in literature, and guide the adults to use a gender justice lens whenever reading children's books in the classroom:

> *Rashawn is a boy in a preschool classroom where gender stereotypes in literature are routinely questioned. One day a new substitute teacher, Jolene, is reading books with the children. Jolene points to a character in an illustration and says, "Look at what she's doing."*
>
> *"How do you know it's a girl?" Rashawn asks.*
>
> *"Because her name is Catherine. Catherine is a girl's name."*
>
> *"No it's not!" says Rashawn. There's no such thing as a girl's name. Because anyone can have any name."*
>
> *Jolene pauses. "You know," she says, "I've never thought about that before, but you're right!"*

Self-study and classroom audit tool: applying a gender justice lens to your library and storytelling

Use the statements below as a guide to think about the ways you interact with children (statements 1–7), families and caregivers (statements 8–20), and other teachers and staff in your program (statements 21–25). If your response to any of these statements is "Of course I do!" we encourage you to think critically about ways you could continue to improve on that area. Nobody is perfect, and we all operate from a position of assumption and bias based on our own experiences, no matter how long we do this work. Consider how children, families, and peers might answer these statements about you as well. There is always room for growth and recognizing this is one of the best things we can do for children!

1. My school library includes books that meaningfully portray characters with diverse gender identities as well as gender expressions that expand, cross, or transcend the traditional male and female binary.

2. My school library includes books that meaningfully portray TGE characters who also have other diverse aspects of their identity represented, for instance, characters of diverse body size, skin tones, and abilities. Additionally, characters who are neurodiverse and/or from diverse cultural backgrounds, ethnicities, religions, class cultures, and economic circumstances.

3. The books in my school library that portray TGE characters explore a wide range of topics and ideas; the plot does not revolve around the characters' gender identity or expression.

4. The books in my school library that portray TGE characters focus on the positive attitudes, beliefs, and behaviors we want children to emulate.

5. My library includes books that introduce a variety of pronouns or use no pronouns throughout the entire book.

6. I apply an "80/20" rule in regards to bullying and other negativity surrounding TGE identities and expressions: 80% of books with TGE characters contain no bullying, rejection, gender policing, internalized transphobia, or other forms or gender bias. Within the 20% of books that do contain these themes, descriptions of these negative and possibly traumatizing events and states comprise no more than 20% of the story.

7. I have applied a gender justice lens to all books in my library. When I find books that reinforce harmful gender stereotypes or binary gender roles, I remove these books from my library, use them as teaching tools to generate discussion about gender stereotypes, or modify the narrative (for example, changing pronouns).

— Chapter 6 —

Working with Families and Colleagues to Support Children's Gender Health and Create Gender Justice in Our Programs

As she has observed Lucien's gender journey over the year, Teacher Heather has become concerned that her school is not doing enough to support Lucien and her family. Heather organized a professional development day for staff with a local organization that does trainings on gender creative children, and it goes well. Next, she organizes a parent education night on the subject. She is pleased to see Lucien's parents on the RSVP list.

Meanwhile, parent–teacher conferences have begun, and Teacher Meg has split the children between the two teachers. Teacher Heather sees that Meg has chosen Lucien's family for herself, and she becomes nervous. Heather has tried to talk to Meg about Lucien's emerging awareness of gender, but Meg talks over her and insists that she knows about gender equality, and refutes Heather's ideas and observations. Heather does not think that Meg is likely to handle the subject with the necessary sensitivity, and asks if she would mind if she traded one of hers for Lucien. Meg seems to feel challenged, and explains that she has known Lucien's family longer, since Lucien's older sibling attended the school a few years before Heather started teaching there, and she thinks it's best if they just stay with her. Heather reluctantly concedes.

As Heather is sweeping the classroom after lunch on Meg's conference day, she looks up and sees Lucien's parents walking out of the conference room. They do not look happy. Meg enters the classroom, her jaw set in anger. "They yelled at me—got upset with me because I started the conference talking about how Lucien is identifying as a girl, and how we told the kids, and they are fine with it!" Heather winces at the use of the word "we." She hopes that they have not completely lost the trust of this family. "Lucien's mom went OFF on me about how the only thing I mentioned is the gender thing, and not how he's doing in all of these other areas—she said it made her feel like the school has an agenda. Anyway, I guess they aren't coming to the parent education night you planned about gender now—I just hope they don't pull Lucien out of this school! She said she was thinking about it."

Heather's heart sank. She had been so close to building a relationship with this family. She had been looking forward to being in partnership with them as they worked together to support this sweet and complex child. And now, between Teacher Meg announcing to the class, "Lucien is a girl now!" and this disastrous conference, it looked like all efforts to embrace Lucien's gender journey had been damaged, at best. Heather knew that Meg didn't do any of this out of cruelty. She wished she had listened to her—and she especially wished Meg had been more attentive during the professional development day—but she knew Meg felt terrible, and didn't know how to fix it.

Caring, attuned relationships are the soil necessary for justice work to grow in any setting. Many of us who teach young children entered the field because we adore them and have a special ability to connect with children in ways that we may not share in our comfort or skill level in relating to other adults. Nevertheless, other adults—including families, co-workers, and administrators—have a significant impact on children's lives, and we must learn to work together effectively if we are to succeed in creating environments that support people of all genders. In this chapter, we discuss the importance of building partnerships with families, navigating difficult conversations, and shifting organizational culture to embrace gender justice where you work.

Children get it. It makes sense to them. But the parents go ballistic! What do I say to the parents? –Workshop Attendee

Working with families and adults: key approaches

Note: Throughout this chapter, we suggest many strategies for communicating with families about gender. Almost everything we discuss ALSO applies to communication with colleagues. We introduce additional approaches to working with colleagues at the end of this chapter.

Build partnerships

Strong partnerships with families are critical for the success of any early childhood program, and we want to bring just as much intention to developing them as we do when we are developing relationships, curriculum, and play spaces inside our classrooms. We want to build trust with families, support them, and encourage them to be advocates and allies working in collaboration with us in this important work. Partnership with families begins by reimagining our own role as teachers and thinking of ourselves as collaborators with families rather than experts who know what's best for their child. Remember there is no single "right way" of enacting gender justice. There are as many ways to support children's gender agency as there are children with their diverse lived experiences and unique intersectional gender constellations.

For some of us, shifting this way of thinking of ourselves from experts to partners can go against deeply held and perhaps unconscious beliefs. To create meaningful partnerships with families, we must recognize and relinquish any beliefs that we are the experts of anyone else's experiences besides our own. To be in true partnership, teachers must become listeners and learn from families. At the same time, we have our own strengths to bring to the partnership, including our unique experiences and positions as teachers, educators, and administrators. Our goal is to create teaching and learning that is reciprocal, acknowledging that both teachers and families have important perspectives about the child that can complement and enhance one another.

In the story with Heather and Meg, we see that while Meg's intentions were to inform Lucien's family of the recent developments in the child's gender identity, her lack of attunement with the parents led to a lot of upset feelings. Perhaps starting the conference with affirmations about how Lucien was doing in many other areas of the classroom, including specific anecdotes that demonstrate that the teachers know and appreciate the whole child, would have established a foundation of trust needed to touch on such a potentially delicate subject as Lucien's exploration of gender.

Take a strength-based approach

Building a responsive, strength-based relationship with families begins by expressing genuine interest in getting to know them and partnering with them to support their child. Remember that families are their children's first advocates and each family knows their child better than anyone but the child themself. Each family has their own family and cultural values, beliefs, and goals that inform how and why they make the parenting/caregiving choices they do. Ask families about the goals and dreams they have for their children, any concerns they have, the forms of support they would like their children to receive, and what they want their children to learn while attending your early childhood program. A strength-based approach in our work with families requires that we begin with a belief that all families have resources, personal characteristics, capacities, and relationships that can be mobilized to enhance their learning and well-being, no matter how many risk factors or challenges they face (Center for the Study of Social Policy, 2018). Honoring each family's strengths, and inviting their knowledge and perspectives to inform how we work with their children, create a foundation for a genuine partnership where we work alongside them rather than on behalf of them.

Meet families where they are in their gender journeys

We cannot have productive dialogue with families or meet them where they are until we tune in to their values, beliefs, cultural routines, feelings, and preferred practices. We can do this by paying attention to what they do and say—not by making assumptions about them based on their culture, religion, race, nationality, or other social category of identity and experience. When a family does hold cultural beliefs that are deeply invested in binary gender roles, we must respect their cultural beliefs and experiences while also establishing inclusive norms inside our classrooms and programs.

Setting a gender justice tone within your program or school community

Nonbinary and expansive approaches to gender are new to many people. We can't wait until something happens to talk about gender with families. Instead, we want to set the tone of gender inclusion from the beginning of our relationship with a child and their family. Here are some strategies for setting a gender-justice tone:

Draft a mission or values statement for your program that clearly expresses a value in human diversity and differences, and a commitment to addressing bias and supporting young children in being justice makers. Share this statement with families as they enter your program or school community.

Example: At our school, we believe that while we all share things in common, it is our differences that make us who we are. We are committed to anti-bias education and righting wrongs in our school community.

As you welcome families to your school, provide resources about the language you plan to use around gender. Solicit feedback, and begin conversations with families who have questions, concerns, and input. Do the same for the language you use to represent other aspects of diversity (e.g., race, diverse family structures, disabilities) that you anticipate may spark questions and concerns among the families in your program. From the reactions you receive, you will be better positioned to decide where families are at and how to support them throughout the year. For example, you may decide it would be helpful to share some informational articles or host a family education night about gender.

> *Last year, I started talking with kids about pronouns and gender during circle time. When that trickled back to parents, a few of them got really upset. This year, I met with my supervisor to explain that I wanted to bring up the topic at parent orientation. I asked for her support to make sure that when I did bring this up with the parents, she was on board. At the orientation I announced: "I am trying something new this year. I will be talking with children about pronouns, and I will be using the words 'queer,' 'straight,' 'trans,' and 'cisgender' to describe adults and families. This is very different from the preschool that I went to, and it is new for me as well as you. What do you think? Would it be helpful if I share the language I use with the children to describe what these words mean?" Some parents did have concerns and questions, but it opened the conversation, and we were able to work through their questions and concerns together. –Valentina, PreK-Teacher*

Share ongoing information with families about topics your class is exploring, including conversations and conflicts that emerge in the classroom around social identities, including around gender. Share the language you use to respond when new discoveries or conflicts about gender arise.

Example excerpt from an email to families: "We have been continuing to talk about our similarities and differences at circle time this week. Here are some of the words the children used to name their gender identities…"

Talking with families about TGE children: helpful approaches

Remember the whole child in conversations with family members. In the story that opens this chapter, Teacher Meg immediately alienates Lucien's parents when she focuses solely on Lucien's gender identity during their parent–teacher conference. Whether or not they support their child's gender agency, families of TGE children also want to know about their child's art, friends, and accomplishments. They want to know how their child is growing physically, cognitively, creatively, and socioemotionally, and they want to know that their child's teachers are paying attention to them across these domains. If we isolate gender as the subject to report on, we risk exaggerating its importance in the life of the child and increasing the alarm of family members. **Instead, we want to treat gender as just one aspect of a child's identity of many that they are currently exploring** as seen in the following example of a preschool teacher's conversation with a parent about their four-year-old child, Ray:

Areas in the classroom your child loves to explore include painting, blocks, and dramatic play. Ray loves to build large structures and often invites other children to join in. I have enclosed a few of Ray's recent paintings. As you can see, there has been much exploration with color and tools—everything from paintbrushes to fingertips to toy cars. Ray also loves playing dress up! Lately Ray has been playing "princesses" with Mona and Jasmine. They put on the sparkly crowns and tutus, and take turns freezing each other with their ice powers.

Take a strengths-based approach when talking about TGE identities and expressions

Think about the positive aspects of children's gender identities and expressions and use them to frame the way you approach the topic. When we treat TGE children as "issues" to be solved, we are doing harm. This approach can cascade for children into deep feelings of shame.

For example, teachers could say: "I noticed that after Pedro came to school in a dress a few weeks ago, lots more boys in the class have tried on dresses and skirts and have also worn them to school. He's really made a difference in what children are comfortable with, and he helped to spread a lot of joy in the classroom!"

> *"It's [being transgender] not just this obstacle in your life that we're gonna have to deal with. It's like, awesome." –Cori, Transgender Preschool Teacher*

Have gender expansive resources on hand

These are useful to offer families (e.g., books, videos, podcasts, organizations, events, and information about local or online support groups). See the resource guide at the end of this book for some suggestions on places to start.

The Both/And stance

One of the major goals is for parents and children to move from an experience of "either/or" to one of "both/and" (Malpas, 2011). Children can both affirm their identity and understand the demands of a world mostly organized around the gender binary. Family members can both nurture their child's unique self and help mediate between the child's wish and the social reality.

Parents and other primary caregivers are typically in the best position to judge a child's safety at home and in the various spaces and communities they move through when they're not at school. As teachers, we cannot eradicate bias and oppression from the child's life, but through our programs, we can offer one safe place for a child to embody their authentic gender self. We can also advocate for the importance of a child having one safe place, so that family members will find ways to create that for their child after they have left our program. Of course, it's not possible to make any place fully safe, but we offer this language as something to aspire to.

Have empathy for all the ways that families are having to navigate this experience with their children. Tune in to what's coming up for family members as they seek to support their children. Even if you don't feel the same way they do, validate their feelings. Remember that adults need to be validated just as much as the children we work with do.

When families are reluctant to embrace gender expansiveness

Just as we need to respect the children in our care, we need to respect the families we work with—even those who may not be on board with a gender expansive classroom culture. How can we "invite in" families who are reluctant to embrace gender expansiveness? Some strategies are detailed below.

"Inviting in" vs. "calling out"

Using the language of Restorative Justice (Van Ness & Strong, 2010), we call it "inviting in" rather than "calling out" when we identify beliefs and reactions from family members that might be causing stress and shame in children. Instead of placing blame on families for behaviors that might be harmful to the gender health of children, we look to include them in co-creating a plan for how we can all best meet the needs of their children as well as all the other children in our care. Telling someone that what they are doing is harmful to their child without first building a foundation of trust, respect, and mutual care for that child, is likely to result in defensiveness and damaged relationships. There are many ways we can work towards a more collaborative and productive dynamic when working with families.

What is Restorative Justice? Restorative Justice (RJ) is a relationship-based approach to building community and handling conflict. It is used often in prisons and in schools and requires a paradigm shift from punitive-based approaches (where harm is viewed through a lens of perpetrator and victim, and responses emphasize blame and punishment) to a healing-based approach. A healing orientation views harm from the perspective of the damage done that impacts relationships and a belief that everyone affected needs support in order to restore healthy relationships.

RJ is rooted in an understanding of human connection and equity with the belief that "Hurt people hurt people." It is a fluid approach, open to changing over time and context to include new voices and adapt to updated values. RJ is intentionally community based, emphasizing shared leadership, personal responsibility, and accountability where every voice is heard and the most affected are also the most respected.

Be thoughtful about who engages upset family members in conversation, and when and where they do it. Our feelings about gender run deep. They are connected to our core belief and value systems, and also our core identities and sense of self. Listening to someone express beliefs that oppose our own beliefs can activate our body's stress response system (fight, flight, or freeze behaviors, as well as the types of resistance we have talked about). While these reactions may help us avoid harm in a life-or-death situation, they unfortunately are not helpful when working through disagreements. All of them tend to either escalate or avoid the conflict. When you feel yourself getting flooded by intense emotions, take a deep breath and then name what you are feeling and request a break: "Oh, I can feel myself starting to get angry. When I'm angry it's hard for me to hear what you're saying, and I really want to know what you think. Can we schedule a time to come back to this conversation?" Remember to keep everyone out of the **danger zone** if possible. Here are a few tips about scheduling a conversation with a family:

- TGE teachers are more directly impacted by transphobic remarks. Cisgender teachers and staff members can support TGE co-workers by volunteering to have these conversations with reluctant or resistant family members (or other co-workers).

- Consider who is the best person to talk to this particular family— is it a teacher? Director? Another family member at your school? This will all depend on the situation and the relationships!

- What is the best way to communicate in this situation? An all-school email? A one-on-one conversation during pick up? A scheduled meeting? It all depends.

Once you have determined who will engage in the conversation, and where and when it will occur, you are ready to communicate. Here are some strategies for successful communication:

- **Establish a shared purpose.** We start this work with the assumption that both teachers and families have a deep commitment to doing what is best for children. We want to see children thrive and grow. This is our shared purpose, and it is a place to begin and return to again and again as we engage in conversations about the strategies we use to make that happen.

- **Begin your work with families around gender with a curious mind.** Ask questions to help understand where the family is coming from and how they see their child. If they have fears about a child's gendered behaviors, it's important to understand exactly what it is they are afraid of and why. Here are some examples of questions Teachers Meg or Heather could have asked Lucien's parents:

  — What does it mean to you that Lucien is wearing different clothes at school than they do at home?

  — What do you think Lucien might be expressing/communicating to you?

  — What about this makes you uncomfortable?

  — What worries you about this behavior? What are you afraid it might mean?

  — What is your goal for Lucien's gender health and happiness?

- **Listen to a family's responses with empathy and reflect back what you hear** so that you can make sure you understand correctly, and so the family members feel that you are actually listening. As we explored in Chapter 2, it is important to listen with your full presence, and with an openness to being changed. Before you move on, address any fears and concerns that come up (see below). Give this listening and reflection process the time it needs before offering your own observations about the child. Ask families, "Can we work together to create a plan that supports your child's health and well-being?" That plan might look different for every TGE child in your care, and it starts with honest collaboration with the child and their family.

- **Note: When practicing empathy, NEVER validate transphobic, homophobic, and other hateful statements that you hear.** Ask questions until you uncover the fears and concerns for the child that lie at the root of those sentiments. Empathize with those underlying concerns. For example, if Melissa's dad says, "How many times do I have to tell you? It's not okay for Melissa to change into school clothes and get dirty. I don't want her looking like a... [fill in with transphobic or homophobic comment]!"

You should NOT say, "I understand not wanting her to look like a X." Instead, you could say, "Can you tell me more about that? I want to understand where you're coming from."

- **Acknowledge the family's fears.** Family members may be scared for their child. They may fear for their health and safety. It's important to build rapport with families that allows them to express their worries openly. Acknowledging these fears provides a foundation for addressing them directly. Parents may fear that their child will be bullied in the immediate future. They may also have fears that reach farther into the future—that their child will be gay and/or transgender, will experience discrimination, or simply won't follow the narrative parents have laid out in their minds. Some families' fears are rooted in religious or cultural beliefs about gender or sexuality. Our job is to help families identify those fears and ground them in what we know today. We can't determine the whole course of a child's life or what will bring them distress or struggle later, but there is plenty of research that shows that not having one's gender identity and expression supported at an early age causes distress and struggle in the moment and beyond. We can help families to frame their fears about gender as being no different than other ways parents worry about their children, and we can support them in figuring out how to support their children today.

- **When parents and family members are able to decrease their own anxiety, they are more capable of interrupting their angry and reactive behavior and differentiating their child's needs from their own.** After this occurs, they can learn to advocate for greater flexibility of gender norms in the social and community contexts where their child spends time (e.g., schools, faith communities, family friends, neighbors; Malpas, 2011). It is helpful to acknowledge that expanding notions of gender is a process and a learning experience that may be more challenging for some than others.

- It is also helpful to remember that **most fears families have about gender come from a place of love and concern for their children.** By focusing on the love and strengths that families already have, and by genuinely listening to what they think and where they are coming from, we can create the conditions needed to give a gentle nudge or introduce a new perspective. It takes a lot of courage for families to dig deeply into what it is they are truly afraid of on topics that break the rules of gender, and it is our job to create a supportive and judgment-free environment for that to happen.

- **When you see someone getting activated by a fight, flight, or freeze stress response, name it.** Just as you can say, "I'm feeling myself starting to withdraw and shut down. Can we schedule a time to talk this weekend? I do want to hear what you're saying and follow up," you can also check-in when you notice this happening in someone else. When you do this with respect and consent, it can help the person gain self-awareness and feel cared for. For example, "Can we pause this conversation for a moment? I notice you're starting to clench your fists supertight. Do you want to tell me about what's coming up for you?"

- One caveat here is that we always want to **check ourselves for tone policing:**[14] this is when one criticizes someone's emotional state so they can ignore and invalidate one's statement or idea. Tone policing is used to protect privilege. It is a frequent tactic used by people with power—such as white folks and cismen—to refuse to listen to what oppressed people—such as people of color, women, and trans folks—are saying, because they're "too angry" or "too emotional." NEVER criticize someone's emotions—validate them! And, practice tuning in to when people cross from the "uncomfortable zone of learning" into their "danger zone." You might say, "This is an important and challenging topic to discuss. I know we both want to be able to really hear one another. Let's take a short break to stretch, take a few deep breaths, or walk around a little. Just stopping to breathe for a minute or two will really help us to stay focused and productive in our conversation together." Communication cannot happen in the danger zone.

- **Always bring it back to your shared purpose: the health of the child.** When families show significant resistance, we can always center discussions around the health of the child. Remind yourself and the family that you are all committed to the same goal. Feeling supported in their gender identity and expression is central to a child's mental and physical health. While as adults we are often seeking certainty and definition, we may need to support children in uncertainty to give them the space and safety they need to explore their identities and expressions. This may increase the family's fears and anxieties, but fear should not be the dominant narrative the child sees and experiences. Children are highly attuned to the emotional states of the adults in their lives, and if they see that their gendered behaviors cause fear and anxiety they will learn to hide who they really are. This creates a breeding ground for shame and self-doubt. While we don't want to scare or shame families into accepting their children, we do want to make sure they know the impact their fears can have on the health of their children if the fear is allowed to dominate.

- **Emphasize child agency.** As we have discussed throughout this book, gender health is optimally supported when teachers and adults focus on attunement and listening to what children are telling us about their genders. It is helpful to have specific observations and things you have heard from the child to relay to family members (see below).

- **Use your school's mission statement and early childhood education standards**, including the National Association for the Education of Young Children's (NAEYC) code of ethics and draft position statement "Advancing Equity in Early Childhood Education" (2018) and the United Nations Convention on the Rights of the Child (UNCRC), to build the case for supporting children's gender agency.

- **Use observations and documentation in communication about gender with families.** Observations and documentation help to create a comprehensive picture of children's experiences, development, and learning, and to support planning meaningful curricula for each child. Because observations guide early childhood teachers to learn about how children think, what their interests are, and how they are making sense of the world, teachers can learn a lot about how a child is understanding and thinking about gender just by closely watching and listening to what they say and do. Teachers' observations can be shared with families to support conversations about the child's experiences at school, including—but not limited to—what a child is communicating to others about gender. Documentation makes children's thinking and learning visible. Teachers can use a variety of documentation methods (e.g., written observations, language samples, children's constructions such as blocks, art, and Lego®), drawings, dictation and writing, photos, audio/video recordings, and learning stories to capture children's thinking and learning about gender. Then they can gather, share, and discuss this information with parents and families.

- **Focus on the current moment—for today and tomorrow— vs. worrying about what today's behaviors mean for a child's future.** What would happen if we listen to your child today? Support families to focus on the immediate moment of their child's experience, and discourage them from trying to identify what a child's behaviors might predict for the future. A teacher might say to a parent: "In early childhood, we don't need to worry about hormones and medical transition for a while yet."

- **Help family members move from helplessness to empowerment.** Family members can experience so much worry for their child that without support and guidance, they can shift into feelings of helplessness. They may not know how to help their child nor the critical role their acceptance plays in their child's self-acceptance, social-emotional health and resilience, and overall well-being (Malpas, 2011). Teachers can reinforce both the importance of attunement and caring relationships for TGE children, and the many ways that caring adults can support, protect, advocate for, acknowledge, respect, and cherish them.

- **Reflect on your own gender biases, experiences, and beliefs and understand how they influence your work with families.** As discussed in Chapter 2, it is essential that teachers consider the attributions and biases they may have about the parents and family members of children in their class.

Talking with families about children's gender biases

It's like this fine line between trying to say something without explicitly saying your child has really got some issues around enforcing who can be what gender. And I don't know where this is coming from, but we do know it's learned. -Kelly Former Preschool Teacher

It's important that we have these conversations with not only families of TGE children but also families of children who are displaying gender bias including bullying, teasing, excluding, or policing each other's gender, and children who are internalizing binary gender roles to the extent that they are limiting themselves in play. In these conversations, most of the communication strategies listed above apply—including talking about the whole child, talking about your observations rather than judgments or conclusions, sharing your concerns, asking questions, listening, establishing shared purpose, and citing your school's mission statement and early childhood standards of care. The goal of these conversations is to find strategies to interrupt and change biased behavior—not only to protect other children in the classroom, but also for the benefit of the child displaying the bias. Bias harms those dishing it out as well as those receiving it. Among other reasons, when children display gender bias they further internalize a binary gender that limits their own ability to grow their capabilities and empathy for others.

Working with colleagues

As mentioned above, these strategies apply to working with colleagues as well as with families. In the following box, a preschool teacher reflects on his process for giving colleagues feedback about gender bias. An important responsibility teachers have is learning how to speak up and say something when you notice gender bias in your program. Silence is easier and more comfortable, but we always have to return to ask ourselves: What is the impact on the children?

Getting colleagues on board with gender justice

We need to establish shared purpose, understanding, and language with our colleagues. Here are some strategies:

- **Read this book as a group! Go through the self-study and classroom audit tool together!** Commit to the process! It can be helpful to create group agreements as you approach this work together.

- **It can be helpful to bring in outside trainers to hold the space for "Gender 101" work.** There is currently only a shortlist of organizations and consultants who provide trainings on gender diversity and who specialize in early childhood; see our website for a list of those who do. Many more people and organizations offer general gender diversity trainings, and good trainers will tailor the training to your workplace needs if you tell them about your situation ahead of time. Asking for resources from your local LGBTQI+ pride center is a good place to start.

- **If you do bring in outside training, make note of who shows up, pays attention, and seems receptive—and who does not.** You can often spot forms of resistance (such as believing one already knows, not feeling the need to know, or needing not to know) at trainings like this. It is not usually productive to call this resistance out publicly, but you can make a note to yourself about how you might invite these folks in over time.

Connecting to practice: a preschool teacher reflects on how he begins conversations about gender with colleagues

When I think about how I work with my colleagues to support them to change how they are thinking about a child, I have a process that I go through. Recently I had to talk to my co-teacher about how she was grouping children:

I notice what's happening. My co-teacher Krystal was excusing the children to wash their hands for lunch. Krystal was alternating "boy-girl-boy-girl."

I ask myself questions:

What did I see? Krystal was organizing the children by binary gender groups.

Why did it stick out to me? This is not acknowledging the gender diversity in our classroom.

What's the impact? A few children seem uncomfortable or unsure about being grouped this way.

What could be her intention or reason for deciding to organize the children this way? Krystal is making hand-washing time into a game.

What could I do to help my colleague accomplish her goal in a less harmful way? I could model other, more inclusive ways to excuse the children.

What is the best way to communicate with Krystal about this? At a meeting? During nap time? When we are planning curriculum? The next time it comes up? I want to talk about it soon, but I know I should wait until there are no children around.

Then I look for, or create, the opportunity to initiate a conversation. I ask Krystal if she can chat for a moment after the children have left for the day.

When I talk with colleagues, I tend to focus on impacts, strategies, strengths, goals, and values, and other ways to accomplish their intentions. I check in with Krystal at the end of the day. I share that grouping children by gender might make some of the children uncomfortable, and I offer some suggestions for other ways to organize them. I tell Krystal that I notice that the children love her games.

With my co-workers, I also work to create an environment where there are routines in place for communication, feedback, and reflection. Krystal and I decide to keep a daily log of our classroom observations and feedback. We will be the only ones who read it, so we can communicate freely. The Daily Log is kept in a drawer, and both of us have a key to the drawer. On our breaks or at the end of the day, we both jot down observations and indicate when we want to talk more about a situation. At our weekly Teacher Meeting, we review the contents of the log, discuss our observations, and develop strategies for how to move forward as a teaching team.

I ask my colleagues to talk about their values related to a topic before it becomes a problem. I asked Krystal if she feels attached to grouping the children by gender, and if so, I ask her why.

I ask my colleagues to tell me when and how they like to receive feedback. I also try to model unpacking a challenging interaction, with the hope that they will do the same. When it is my turn to dismiss the children to wash hands, I call the children by details on their clothes. One child tells another that they can't be a boy if their shoes have pink gems on them. I facilitate a conversation between the children, and ask questions to determine why the child thinks this. Krystal jumps in and asks the children if sparkles are a boy thing, a girl thing, or an everyone thing. The class votes, with the majority in favor of "everybody."

Another thing I tend to do is try to pre-plan what I could say in common situations that arise in a classroom with young children. Let's say, for example, that I know when someone is going to read Mo Willem's (2003) book *Time to PEE!*, about going to the bathroom; it says "Boys can stand up and girls should sit." I will have a few things in mind to say, like "I usually read that some people stand up and some people sit. Different people can do different things."

When it comes to a teacher's behavior that is hurtful for a child, I may struggle saying something in the moment. I will often find a less emotionally charged time to focus on sharing strategies. When I am calm, I share with Krystal: "I don't tend to use the term 'boys' or 'girls' in the classroom because I want to do what I can to avoid the self-segregation that tends to happen for children. It seems like the less we group them by gender, the less they expect it to happen. Have you observed the same thing?"

Another strategy I use is to give feedback that is focused on what happened and the impact on the children. I shared my observations with Krystal and asked her to notice the expressions of certain children when gender assignments occur. I also read some anecdotes from my observation journal. Krystal said that she has not noticed these things, but agreed to be more mindful in her language. Before I spoke to Krystal, I asked her if it was a good time for feedback and, when she said it was, I began by sharing what I thought her intention was. In this case, I told her that I could see that the children enjoyed playing games when they are being excused during transitions, and that her big personality and sense of humor always make it fun for the children. It's like I'm saying to Krystal, "I see you and I also see this."

Gender justice among colleagues: the administrative level

A teacher started having a conversation with a parent of a TGE child at pick-up time. I don't think the teacher was totally clear about the administration having her back and being in support of it, so wasn't aware of what resources might have been available. It did not go well. I think if we had been much clearer as a school and been able to rely on director support more, she could have maybe asked the parent, "Let's have this conversation with the director and not right now," and maybe the outcome would have been different. –Toby, former Preschool Teacher

Support from directors and administrative leadership makes an enormous difference in teachers' ability to support and advocate for children's gender health—as well as in creating positive working conditions for TGE teachers and employees. While we do not have space in this book to explore gender justice at an administrative level, we do have a list of recommendations, printed as a checklist, in our audit tool below. Watch our website for future updates on administrator resources, and in the meantime, take a look at the resources produced by Gender Spectrum for use in K–12 environments. Many of their downloadable documents can be adapted to suit the needs of early childhood programs.

Self-study and classroom audit tool: relationships and interactions with families and colleagues

Use the statements below as a guide to think about the ways you interact with families (statements 1–13) and other teachers and staff in your program (statements 13–18). If your response to any of these statements is "Of course I do!" we encourage you to think critically about ways you could continue to improve on that area. Nobody is perfect, and we all operate from a position of assumption and bias based on our own experiences, no matter how long we do this work! Consider how children, families, and peers might answer these statements about you as well. There is always room for growth and recognition that this is one of the best things we can do for children.

1. I treat parents and family members with respect. I pay attention to what family members do and say, and value their contributions to the classroom.

2. I take the time to ask/learn from families about their family structures, traditions, and norms. I stay respectful and stay curious.

3. I am willing to adjust my curriculum each year in response to the needs of families.

4. I provide resources about the language I plan to use around gender at the beginning of the year, solicit feedback, and begin conversations with families who have questions, concerns, and input.

5. I approach relationships with families as partnerships in supporting the gender health and growth of their children together.

6. I resist holding the role of "expert" in how children should experience or do gender.

7. I communicate a holistic awareness of each child, remembering that gender identity is just one aspect of a child, not their whole being. When I talk with families I tell them many things about their child. I do not focus exclusively on gender.

8. I introduce families to gender diversity resources.

9. I share ongoing information about read-alouds, conversations, and conflicts that emerge in the classroom around gender, including the language I use to respond.

10. When conflicts arise, I listen to family members' opinions and feelings without judgment. I validate these feelings and attempt to uncover underlying motivations.

11. I talk about the strengths that come from children's gender expressions and identities rather than "problems" associated with them.

12. I advocate for children's gender health and well-being.

13. I utilize the support I have (school mission, NAEYC professional code of ethics) in enacting my professional responsibility to address gender justice with colleagues and families.

14. I instigate and encourage discussion about children's gender exploration with my co-workers.

15. I work to create a classroom culture in which teachers communicate with and understand one another about approach to gender.

16. I foster continuity and consistency in the way teachers respond to children's gender exploration.

17. I use methods of observation and documentation to reflect on children's gender exploration, taking notice of language they use to describe

themselves and each other. I share and discuss my observations with my co-workers.

18. I solicit feedback and support from students, parents, and colleagues on how my gender bias shows up in the classroom, recognizing that this is an ongoing process.

Self-study and classroom audit tool: admin and HR considerations

1. My school has a mission or values statement that clearly expresses a value in human diversity and differences.

2. My school has a mission or values statement that expresses a commitment to addressing injustice and supporting young children in being justice makers.

3. Our family intake forms use gender-neutral words like "family members" instead of "mother and father." Forms are inclusive of diverse family structures, and flexible about the numbers of primary caregivers in a child's life.

4. Family intake forms allow parents/guardians to express their own and their child's gender in their own words, beyond binary F/M choices. Forms include opportunities to share someone's preferred name.

5. Diversity, including gender diversity, is celebrated among teachers and staff and viewed as valuable in hiring decisions. At the same time, teachers and staff are conscious about not tokenizing members of marginalized identities.

6. HR practices are inclusive of TGE employees, and administration has taken care to put in place gender-inclusive policies (see Transgender Law Center link on our Resources page).

7. School provides professional development resources to support employees' continual learning and development, including ongoing education about gender diversity by people and/or organizations with this expertise.

8. Administrators partner with teachers, families, and children to develop individualized game plans for supporting transgender and gender

expansive children. Focus is given to respecting children's wishes around names, pronouns, whether or not a child is "out" to other children and faculty/staff, and other administrative and logistical factors.

9. Program policies do not limit teachers' interactions with children based on the gender of the teacher.

Where Have We Come From and Where Are We Going Now?

The only way I will rest in peace is if one day transgender people aren't treated the way I was: they're treated like humans, with valid feelings and human rights. Gender needs to be taught about in schools, the earlier the better. My death needs to mean something. My death needs to be counted in the number of transgender people who commit suicide this year. I want someone to look at that number and say "That's f****d up" and fix it. Fix society. Please. –From the suicide note of Leelah Alcorn, 17-year-old transgender girl

Leelah, the same young person who cried tears of joy when she learned the word "transgender" because she finally understood who she was, left this world just three short years later. But she also left us instructions. She told us that gender needs to be taught about in schools—the earlier the better.

To do the work of gender justice right, we need to grapple with the hard truth of bias, oppression, and hate, and the impact it has on young children (and the rest of us). We said from the start that this work must go beyond the level of inclusion by being actively anti-oppression, or we will not truly be working towards justice for young people like Leelah. And we need to do this with children right from the start. The earlier the better.

We cannot put the burden of beginning this work on the children who need our support to thrive, and who may already be hiding from us. It is our responsibility to fight for the day when we can say that the last child has been lost to hate and fear and shame.

My family loves and supports me... [but] I don't think they
necessarily prepared the world for me as much as they were trying
to prepare me for the world.[15] *–Jen, nonbinary adult*

In early childhood education, we have the opportunity to flip the script. We have the chance to stop forcing children into the ready-made gender boxes of this world and to start demanding that the world stretch, shift, and expand to make room for the beauty that is gender diversity and the creativity that children can bring to it. We must start asking ourselves what we can do to prepare the world for children, instead of the other way around.

When we consider the vast scale and reach of the gender binary it is easy to feel hopeless about making change. We may have influence in our program, but what about the constant messages a child is bombarded with by the media and society every day? What about when they go off to kindergarten? When we feel overwhelmed by the omnipresence of gender bias in the world, we can remind ourselves that we do have power to make a change. Even if that change is as small as one child having an adult at a formative time in their life, who sees and supports their whole self, it is valuable. A relatively small change in our language, curriculum, or awareness could make the difference between isolation and joy in a child's gender experiences. Encian asks, "How would my life have been different if I had seen myself reflected in one book as a young child? Sure, it's just one person's life—but for me, my life is everything!"

A theory of change currently rippling through social justice communities, called **emergent strategy**, tells us: "Emergence is the way complex systems and patterns arise out of a multiplicity of relatively simple interactions" (Brown, 2017, p. 3, quoting Obolensky, 2014). In other words, our small-scale actions combine into complex patterns that we can't see from our vantage points but which could very well create a tipping point for gender justice. According to emergent strategy, **"small is good, small is all"** (Brown, 2017, p.41).

While it is these small-scale changes that we focus on in this book— gender justice via child's agency, interpersonal relationships with children and families, and creating gender inclusive programs in which children recognize gender bias and advocate for themselves and others—our actions can build momentum for large-scale change. Much like **emergent listening**, we must be open to being affected AND to how we can affect others and the world. It is also crucial that we keep the larger picture in mind as we engage in this work. **If we listen deeply enough to children, and practice amplifying their voices, the world will have to listen and shape itself into a more just and loving place for people of all genders.** It can be hard to feel empowered to create change on a systemic scale, but through many simple interactions, complex systems and patterns arise. Justice emerges.

We can also extend our impact by remembering to share resources (including financial resources!) when we have an excess, and activating our networks when we have a need. Our individual small-scale changes can be linked together through our communities and connections with other gender advocates to foster a web of gender justice and generations of children who are equipped to change the world.

> *And there's healing and there's joy and play and celebration in gender. This isn't a serious, horrible oppression topic. This is also like, who do we get to be? What do we get to imagine? –Kate, Early Childhood Equity Trainer*

And through justice, we find joy and elation. We have the unique privilege of working with some of the most imaginative, joyful, inventive, and loving people on earth—young children! While we must tackle the injustice that exists in the world, we can simultaneously revel in the freedom created through diversity, love, and respect.

This work is hard but spectacularly rewarding. How often do we get to imagine a new world, and then go out and build it together? Many people, as they first hear about breaking down the gender binary, struggle to imagine what might take its place—three genders? No genders? Gender chaos and confusion?!

What we imagine is a world of gender agency, gender health, gender diversity, and freedom. We imagine a world of love, respect, and justice. What can you imagine? What do your children imagine? Let's go make it a reality!

References

Adams, M., & Zuniga, X. (2016) "Getting Started: Core Concepts for Social Justice Education." In M. Adams and L. Bell (eds) *Teaching for Diversity and Social Justice* (pp. 95–130). New York, NY: Routledge.

Agosto, D. (2016) "Why storytelling matters: unveiling literary benefits of storytelling." *Association for Library Services to Children*, 14(2), 21–26.

Alcorn, L. (2014, December 31) "Listen to Leelah Alcorn's final words." Retrieved from *Slate*. Accessed on January 22, 2019 at http://www.slate.com/blogs/outward/2014/12/31/leelah_alcorn_transgender_teen_from_ohio_should_be_honored_in_death.html

Auer, P. (ed.). (1998) *Language, Interaction, and Identity*. New York, NY: Routledge.

Bishop, R. S. (1990) "Mirrors, windows, and sliding glass doors." Originally published in *Perspectives*, 1(3), ix–xi. Accessed on January 22, 2019 at https://scenicregional.org/wp-content/uploads/2017/08/Mirrors-Windows-and-Sliding-Glass-Doors.pdf

Blaise, M., & Taylor, A. (2012) "Using queer theory to rethink gender equity in early childhood education." *Young Children*, 67(1), 88.

Broadwell, M. M. (1969) "Teaching for learning (XVI.)." *The Gospel Guardian*, 20(41), 1–3.

Brown, B. (2007) *I Thought It Was Just Me (But It Isn't): Making the Journey from "What Will People Think?" to "I Am Enough."* New York: Penguin.

Brown, B. (June 2010) *The Power of Vulnerability* [video file]. Accessed on January 22, 2019 at http://www.ted.com/talks/brene_brown_on_vulnerability?language=en

Brown, B. (2015) *Daring Greatly: How the Courage to be Vulnerable Transforms the Way We Live, Love, Parent, and Lead*. New York: Penguin.

Brown, A. (2017) *Emergent Strategy: Shaping Change, Changing Worlds*. Chico, CA: AK Press.

California Department of Education (CDE). (2016) "The Integrated Nature of Learning: Best Practices for Planning Curriculum for Young Children." Sacramento, CA: CDE Press. Accessed on January 22, 2019 at https://www.cde.ca.gov/sp/cd/re/documents/intnatureoflearning2016.pdf

Center for the Study of Social Policy. (2018) "The Strengthening Families 101." Accessed on January 22, 2019 at https://cssp.org/resource/strengtheningfamilies101/

Crenshaw, K. (1989) "Demarginalizing the intersection of race and sex: a Black feminist critique of antidiscrimination doctrine, feminist theory, and antiracist politics." *University of Chicago Legal Forum*, 14, 538–554.

Crenshaw, K. W. (1991) "Mapping the margins: intersectionality, identity politics, and violence against women of color." *Stanford Law Review*, 43, 1241–1299.

Daly, L., & Beloglovsky, M. (2018) *Loose Parts 3: Inspiring Culturally Sustainable Environments.* St. Paul, MN: Redleaf Press.

Davies, B. (2014) *Listening to Children: Being and Becoming.* New York: Routledge.

Derman-Sparks, L. N. & Olsen Edwards, J. (2010) *Anti-Bias Education for Young Children and Ourselves* (2nd ed.). Washington, DC: National Association for the Education of Young Children.

de Vries, A. L., & Cohen-Kettenis, P. T. (2012) "Clinical management of gender dysphoria in children and adolescents: the Dutch approach." *Journal of Homosexuality*, 59(3), 301–320.

Dray, B. J., & Wisneski, D. B. (2011) "Mindful reflection as a process for developing culturally responsive practices." *Teaching Exceptional Children*, 44(1), 28–36.

Dykstra, L. (2005) "Trans-friendly preschool." *Journal of Gay & Lesbian Issues in Education*, 3(1), 7–13, doi: 10.1300/J367v03n01_03

Edwards, C., Gandini, L., & Forman, G. (eds). (2011) *The Hundred Languages of Children: The Reggio Emilia Experience in Transformation* (3rd ed.). Santa Barbara, CA: Praeger Publishers.

Ehrensaft, D. (2016a) "Contemporary Understandings of Gender Development." Lecture at Mills College, Oakland, CA.

Ehrensaft, D. (2016b) *The Gender Creative Child: Pathways for Nurturing and Supporting Children Who Live Outside of Gender Boxes.* New York, NY: Experiment Books.

Fast, A. A., & Olson, K. R. (2017) "Gender development in transgender preschool children." *Child Development*, 89(2), 620–637.

Fausto-Sterling, A. (2000) *Sexing the Body: Gender Politics and the Construction of Sexuality.* New York, NY: Basic Books.

Gender Spectrum. (2017) "The Language of Gender." Accessed on January 22, 2019 at https://www.genderspectrum.org/staging/wp-content/uploads/2018/04/Language-of-Gender_3.29.17.pdf

Gonzalez, M. & McNulty, J. (2010) "Achieving competency with transgender youth: school counselors as collaborative advocates." *Journal of LGBT Issues in Counseling*, 4, 176–186. Accessed on January 22, 2019 at http://dx.doi.org/10.1080/15538605.2010.524841

Grieshaber, S., & McArdle, F. (2010) *The Trouble with Play.* London. Open University Press.

Halim, M. L., & Ruble, D. (2010) "Gender Identity and Stereotyping in Early and Middle Childhood." In J. C. Chrisler & D. R. McCreary (eds) *Handbook of Gender Research in Psychology* (pp. 495–525). New York, NY: Springer.

Halim, M. L. D., Bryant, D., & Zucker, K. J. (2016) "Early Gender Development in Children and Links with Mental and Physical Health." In M. R. Korin (ed.) *Health Promotion for Children and Adolescents* (pp. 191–213). Boston, MA: Springer.

Harry, B., & Klingner, J. (2006) *Why Are so Many Minority Students in Special Education? Understanding Race and Disability in Schools.* New York, NY: Teachers College Press.

Haven, K. (2007) *Story Proof: The Science Behind the Startling Power of Story.* Exeter: Libraries Unlimited Press.

Hawkins, D. (2011) *"Malaguzzi's Story, Other Stories, and Respect for Children."* In C. Edwards, L. Gandini, & G. Forman (eds) *The Hundred Languages of Children: The Reggio Emilia Approach: Advanced Reflections* (3rd ed.) (pp. 73–80). Santa Barbara, CA: Praeger.

Hidalgo, M. A., Ehrensaft, D., Tishelman, A. C., Clark, L. F., Garofalo, R., Rosenthal, S. M., & Olson, J. (2013) "The gender affirmative model: what we know and what we aim to learn." *Human Development,* 56(5), 285–290.

Inhelder, B. & Piaget, J. (1958) "The growth of logical thinking from childhood to adolescence.: An essay on the construction of formal operational structures." New York: Basic Books.

James, S. E., Herman, J. L., Rankin, S., Keisling, M., Mottet, L., & Anafi, M. (2016) *The Report of the 2015 U.S. Transgender Survey.* Washington, DC: National Center for Transgender Equality.

Kendall, F. E. (1996) *Diversity in the Classroom: New Approaches to the Education of Young Children.* New York, NY: Teachers College Press.

Keo-Meier, C., & Ehrensaft, D. (2018) *The Gender Affirmative Model: An Interdisciplinary Approach to Supporting Transgender and Gender Expansive Children.* Washington, DC: American Psychological Association.

Kersten, J., Apol, L., & Pataray-Ching, J. (2007) "Exploring the role of children's literature in the 21st-century classroom." *Language Arts,* 84(3), 286.

Kohlberg, L. (1966) "A Cognitive-Developmental Analysis of Children's Sex-Role Concepts and Attitudes." In E. E. Maccoby (ed.) *The Development of Sex Differences* (pp. 82–173). Stanford, CA: Stanford University Press.

Levine, P., & Kline, M. (2007) *Trauma Through a Child's Eyes: Awakening the Ordinary Miracle of Healing; Infancy through Adolescence.* Berkeley, CA: North Atlantic Books.

Lubsen, J. (2012) "Mental Health Disparities Impacting the LGBT Community" (PowerPoint presentation).

Luckner, J. L., & Nadler, R. S. (1997) *Processing the Experience: Strategies to Enhance and Generalize Learning.* Dubuque, IA: Kendall/Hunt Publishing Company.

MacDonald, M. R. (1993) *Storyteller's Start-Up Book: Finding, Learning, Performing, and Using Folktales.* Little Rock, AR: August House.

MacDonald, M. R., Whitman, J., & Whitman, N. (2013) *Teaching with Story: Classroom Connections to Storytelling.* Little Rock, AR: August House.

Mallon, G. P., & DeCrescenzo, T. (2006) "Transgender children and youth: a child welfare practice perspective." *Child Welfare,* 85(2), 215–241.

Malpas, J. (2011) "Between pink and blue: a multi-dimensional family approach to gender nonconforming children and their families." *Family Process,* 50(4), 453–470. Accessed on January 23, 2019 at https://doi.org/10.1111/j.1545-5300.2011.01371.x

Medina, J. (2013) *The Epistemology of Resistance: Gender and Racial Oppression, Epistemic Injustice, and Resistant Imaginations.* New York, NY: Oxford University Press.

Miller, S. (2017) *Princess Hair.* New York: Little, Brown.

Nathanson, D. L. (1994) *Shame and Pride: Affect, Sex, and the Birth of the Self.* London: WW Norton & Company.

National Association for the Education of Young Children (NAEYC) (2018) "Advancing Equity and Diversity in Early Childhood Education: A Position Statement of the National Association for the Education of Young Children." Accessed on January 23, 2019 at https://www.naeyc.org/sites/default/files/globally-shared/downloads/PDFs/resources/position-statements/5-23-18_initial_public_draft_naeyc_equity_statement_0.pdf

Nicholson, S. (1971) "How NOT to cheat children: the theory of loose parts." *Landscape Architecture*, 62, 30–34. Accessed on January 23, 2019 at https://media.kaboom.org/docs/documents/pdf/ip/Imagination-Playground-Theory-of-Loose-Parts-Simon-Nicholson.pdf

Núñez, A. M. (2014). Employing multilevel intersectionality in educational research: Latino identities, contexts, and college access. *Educational Researcher, 43*(2), 85-92.

Obolensky, N. (2014) *Complex Adaptive Learning: Embracing Paradox and Uncertainty* (2nd ed.). New York, NY: Taylor and Francis.

Olsen Edwards, J. (2017) "How to get started with anti-bias education in your classroom and program." *Childcare Exchange*, January/February, 78–82. Accessed on January 23, 2019 at http://www.antibiasleadersece.com/wp-content/uploads/2017/03/How-to-Get-Started-JOE-Final.pdf

Paley, V. (1990) *The Boy Who Would Be a Helicopter*. Cambridge, MA: Harvard University Press.

Paley, V. (1992) *You Can't Say You Can't Play*. Cambridge, MA: Harvard University Press.

Paley, V. (2004) *A Child's Work: The Importance of Fantasy Play*. Chicago, IL: University of Chicago Press.

Panicucci, J. (2007) "Cornerstones of adventure education." In D. Prouty, J. Panicucci, & R. Collinson (eds.), *Adventure Education: Theory and Applications* (pp. 33–48). Champaign, IL: Human Kinetics.

Payne, E., & Smith, M. (2014) "The big freak out: educator fear in response to the presence of transgender elementary school students." *Journal of Homosexuality*, 61(3), 399–418.

Perry, B. D. (2013) "Bonding and attachment in maltreated children." *Child Trauma Center*, 3, 1–17.

Petty, K. (2010) *Developmental Milestones of Young Children*. St. Paul, MN: Red Leaf Press.

Phillips, L. (2000) "Storytelling: the seeds of children's creativity." *Australian Journal of Early Childhood*, 25(3), 1–5.

Pyne, J. (2014) "Gender-independent kids: a paradigm shift in approaches to gender non-conforming children." *Canadian Journal of Human Sexuality*, 23(1), 1–8.

Quinn, P. C., Yahr, J., Kuhn, A., Slater, A. M., & Pascalis, O. (2002) "Representation of the gender of human faces by infants: a preference for female." *Perception,* 31(9), 1109–1121.

Rinaldi, C. (2012) "The Pedagogy of Listening: The Listening Perspectives from Reggio Emilia." In C. Edwards, L. Gandini, & G. Forman (eds) *The Hundred Languages of Children: The Reggio Emilia Approach: Advanced Reflections* (3rd ed.) (pp. 73–80). Santa Barbara, CA: Praeger.

Sensoy, O., & DiAngelo, R. (2017) *Is Everyone Really Equal? An Introduction to Key Concepts in Social Justice Education* (2nd ed.). New York, NY: Teachers College Press.

Smith, A., & Pastel, E. (2018) "Loaded language." Accessed on January 23, 2019 at https://drive.google.com/file/d/1eUosnwYEbImut9nWZONJ-xQuncmajWls/view?usp=drivesdk

Souto-Manning, M. (2013) *Multicultural Teaching in the Early Childhood Classroom: Approaches, Strategies and Tools, Preschool–2nd grade.* New York, NY: Teachers College Press.

Steele, K. (2016) "Looking Back and Looking Forward: An Inquiry into the Lived Experiences of Trans Adults as Young Children." Unpublished manuscript. Mills College, Oakland, CA.

Steensma, T. D., Biemond, R., de Boer, F., & Cohen-Kettenis, P. T. (2011) "Desisting and persisting gender dysphoria after childhood: a qualitative follow-up study." *Clinical Child Psychology and Psychiatry,* 16(4), 499–516.

Steensma, T. D., McGuire, J. K., Kreukels, B. P., Beekman, A. J., & Cohen-Kettenis, P. T. (2013) "Factors associated with desistence and persistence of childhood gender dysphoria: a quantitative follow-up study." *Journal of the American Academy of Child & Adolescent Psychiatry,* 52(6), 582–590.

Steinberg, Z., & Kraemer, S. (2010) "Cultivating a culture of awareness: nurturing reflective practices in the NICU." *ZERO to THREE,* 31(2), 15–22.

Stern, D. (1985) *The Interpersonal World of the Infant.* New York, NY: Basic Books.

Sturm, B. (1999) "The enchanted imagination: storytelling's power to entrance listeners." *School Library Media Research,* 2, 1–21.

Sue, D. W. (2010) "Microaggressions, Marginality, and Oppression: An Introduction." In Sue, D. W. (ed.) *Microaggressions and Marginality: Manifestation, Dynamics, and Impact* (pp. 3–22). Hoboken, NJ: John Wiley & Sons.

Tatum, B. D. (1997) *Why Are All the Black Kids Sitting Together in the Cafeteria? And Other Conversations About Race.* New York, NY: Basic Books.

Taylor, T. F. (2015) "The influence of shame on posttrauma disorders: have we failed to see the obvious?" *European Journal of Psychotraumatology,* 6(1), 28847.

Terry, H. (2012) *How Am I Supposed to Talk About That? Enacting Anti-Racist Pedagogy in Early Childhood Classrooms.* Dubuque, IA: Kendall Hunt Publishing.

Thomas, M. (2013) *Free to Be…You and Me.* Philadelphia, PA: Running Press Kids.

Trimmer, C. (2018) *Teddy's Favorite Toy.* New York, NY: Atheneum Books for Young Readers.

Unger, T. A. (2015) "Learning Truths: Early Childhood Experiences of Gender-Expansive Children and Their Families." Unpublished master's thesis, Mills College, Oakland, CA.

Van Ness, D. & Strong, K. (2010) *Restoring Justice: An Introduction to Restorative Justice* (4th ed.). New Province, NJ: Matthew Bender & Co.

Willems, M. (2003) *Time to PEE!* New York, NY: Hyperion Books for Children.

Wood, J. L. (2018) "Week 1, Part 2—Policing and Schooling Black Boys and Men" [video file]. Accessed on January 23, 2019 at https://youtu.be/BRy5uTBWJ18

Zayed, M. A. A. (nd) "Human Karyotype Training Course Manual." Islamic University of Gaza. Accessed on January 23, 2019 at https://docplayer.net/26273401-Islamic-university-of-gaza-human-karyotype-training-course-manual-prepared-by-mazen-ali-abo-zayed.html

Zosuls, K. M., Ruble, D. N., Tamis-Lemonda, C. S., Shrout, P. E., Bornstein, M. H., & Greulich, F. K. (2009) "The acquisition of gender labels in infancy: implications for gender-typed play." *Developmental Psychology*, 45(3), 688–701. doi: 10.1037/a0014053

Zucker, K. J., Bradley, S. J., Owen-Anderson, A., Kibblewhite, S. J., & Cantor, J. M. (2008) "Is gender identity disorder in adolescents coming out of the closet?" *Journal of Sex & Marital Therapy*, 34(4), 287–290.

Resources

Organizations

Gender Spectrum

https://www.genderspectrum.org

Gender Spectrum provides a range of resources for teens, parents, teachers, and practitioners working with LGBTQ+ individuals including online support groups, webinars, and advocacy resources.

GLSEN

https://www.glsen.org

GLSEN is an education-based organization striving to create inclusive and safe classrooms for K–12 students and teachers regardless of gender and sexual orientation. They provide resources, curriculums, and programs for teachers while engaging in primary research and policy work. Their efforts focus on the four pillars of safety, respect, health, and leadership.

Queerly Elementary

https://queerlyelementary.com

Queerly Elementary provides services and resources to help school communities embrace lesbian, gay, bisexual, transgender and queer diversity.

PFLAG (Parents, Families and Friends of Lesbians and Gays)

https://www.pflag.org

PFLAG brings together LGBTQ+ and their allies in the pursuit of advancing equality through support, education, and advocacy, and provides resources for members and the public.

Transgender Law Center (TLC)

https://transgenderlawcenter.org

The Transgender Law Center (TLC) is the largest national trans-led organization advocating self-determination for all people. Grounded in legal expertise and committed to racial justice, TLC employs a variety of community-driven strategies to keep transgender and gender nonconforming people alive, thriving, and fighting for liberation.

TSER (Trans Student Educational Resources)

http://www.transstudent.org

As a youth-led organization, Trans Student Educational Resources is dedicated to transforming the educational environment for trans and gender nonconforming students through advocacy and empowerment. TSER offers many resources including graphics, workshops, and leadership training.

Non-Organizations

The Gender Wheel

http://www.mayagonzalez.com/blog/2018/03/gender-month-week-one-nature

www.genderwheel.com

Maya Gonzalez, author/illustrator, provides holistic educational tools and curriculum to understand gender.

Queer Kid Stuff

https://queerkidstuff.com

Queer Kid Stuff offers a portal for children and one for parents. The kids' portal offers YouTube videos exploring queer kids' experiences and explaining larger themes children may engage in. The parents' portal provides a range of resources about LGBTQ+ children and youth.

Additional and current resources

Gender Justice in Early Childhood

https://www.genderjusticeinearlychildhood.com/resources/

Gender Justice in Early Childhood is a collective of transgender individuals and allies with experience in early childhood education, research, mental health, and more. We came together to address a growing need for a radical shift in how gender is taught and supported for very young children, in order to create a more just and equitable world. Our goal is to help make expansive understandings of gender accessible and actionable for all teachers of young children.

Endnotes

1   Source: https://www.nytimes.com/2018/10/21/us/politics/transgender-trump-administration-sex-definition.html

2   Source: http://avp.org/wp-content/uploads/2018/01/a-crisis-of-hate-january-release-12218.pdf (page 7).

3   https://en.oxforddictionaries.com/usage/assume-or-presume

4   https://en.wikipedia.org/wiki/Hijra_(Indian_subcontinent)

5   https://thequeerness.com/2017/08/20/the-hijra-community-and-the-complex-path-to-decolonising-gender-in-bangladesh/

6   https://www.intersexequality.com/how-common-is-intersex-in-humans

7   For an in-depth look at how the US medical community treats intersex infants and their families, see the 2017 Human Rights Campaign report: "*I Want to Be Like Nature Made Me.*" https://www.hrw.org/report/2017/07/25/i-want-be-nature-made-me/medically-unnecessary-surgeries-intersex-children-us

8   http://www.isna.org/faq/frequency

9   Source: https://yri.youthradio.org/intheirownwords/p/Jen

10   Our use of "spokes" representing intersecting identities is inspired by Anthias's Multilevel Model of Intersectionality adapted by Nuñez (2014).

11 **Limitations to research:** Gender research continues to develop with new studies and information coming out weekly. However, a critical review of the current literature highlights several limitations. These include: (a) **Old measures**—several of the most highly cited and recent studies rely on out-of-date measures. For example, in Fast and Olsen's 2017 article, which is part of a larger study with additional information coming out, measures used were dated, asking participants if they wanted to be a mommy or daddy when they grow up. (b) **Research populations**—TGE research reflects a small sample of the population, and many studies rely on self-identified TGE families. While this should not deter a reader from the outcomes of the research, it needs to be mentioned that small populations may not reflect the whole of all TGE and each case/experience will be different. (c) **Definitions**—as research continues to expand regarding TGE children, definitions continue to develop and evolve. However, many researchers do not clearly define terms, making some takeaways hard to understand/apply to other situations. and (d) **Most research ignores/dismisses children 0–5 years old**, believing firmly that children that young are incapable of understanding their gender identity.

12 https://www.bbc.com/news/av/magazine-40936719/gender-specific-toys-do-you-stereotype-children

13 https://www.quora.com/How-do-you-refer-to-gender-neutral-and-trans-relatives-Most-words-like-aunt-uncle-and-niece-nephew-are-binary

14 https://everydayfeminism.com/2015/12/tone-policing-and-privilege

15 https://yri.youthradio.org/intheirownwords/c/coming-out

Subject Index

Author Index